❖ DINING **THE CULINARY INSTITUTE OF AMERICA** SERIES ❖

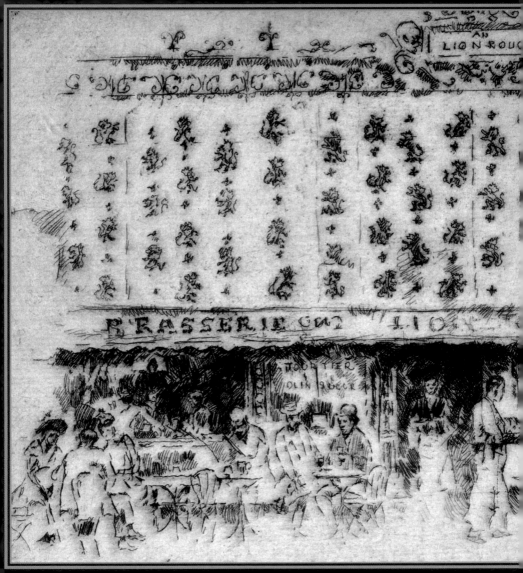

BSINTHE
EXTRA-SUPÉRIEURE
J. ÉDOUARD PERNOT
SOCIÉTÉ ANONYME
ONTBÉLIARD (Doubs)

APÉRITIF
Dans tous les Cafés

BISTROS AND

RECIPES AND REFLECTIONS

JOHN W. FISCHER AND LOU JONES
THE CULINARY INSTITUTE OF AMERICA

Photography by Ben Fink

OF AMERICA DINING SERIES

BRASSERIES

ON Classic Café Cooking

LEBHAR-FRIEDMAN BOOKS

NEW YORK • CHICAGO • LOS ANGELES • LONDON • PARIS • TOKYO

LIBRARY OF CONGRESS CATALOGING-IN-PUBLICATION DATA

Cataloging-in-publication data for this title is on file with the Library of Congress.

ISBN 978-0-86730-924-9

THE CULINARY INSTITUTE OF AMERICA

President: Dr. Tim Ryan

Vice-President, Continuing Education: Mark Erickson

Director of Intellectual Property: Nathalie Fischer

Editorial Project Manager: Mary Donovan

Recipe Testing Manager: Maggie Wheeler

LEBHAR-FRIEDMAN BOOKS

A company of Lebhar-Friedman, Inc., 425 Park Avenue, New York, New York 10022

Publisher: Maria Tufts

Art Director: Kevin Hanek

Manufactured in Singapore on acid-free paper

Table of Contents

As PROFESSORS AT the nation's most prestigious culinary college, we both work diligently at our professional development. We take classes, like other career professionals, attend workshops, and conferences. The thing is, when you work at a college where cuisine is everybody's "major," you have to spend time learning something a little deeper and a littler "truer" about the world of food and wine. To that end, we both took a *Tour Gastronomique de France* in the winter of 2004, covering 2000 kilometers in seven days.

It all started with hopes of introducing a simpler, quicker lunch menu that was still undeniably French. The foods and ambience of bistros and brasseries seemed the obvious place for us to look for inspiration. The two of us love the rich, rustic flavors, and we are not alone.

We worked our way around the countryside, joined by friends and colleagues along the way to share in this one-of-a-kind culinary adventure. We stopped at the restaurants, markets, and wineries of Burgundy, Lyons, Brittany, Loire, Gascony, Champagne, and Paris. We sampled freshly harvested seafood, unctuous cheeses, lively wines, and marvelous, robust fare. In short, we had a fabulous time.

Since our return, we have worked hard to bring a bit of the sensibility we discovered there to our classrooms—John in the dining room and Lou in the kitchen of the college's Escoffier Room Restaurant. We offered a series of special luncheons as part of a Winter Dining Series in our restaurant with menus derived both from our experiences in France and two lifetimes spent learning about and loving bistro fare. The recipes in this book were written for those menus, and we've added to that cache of recipes by developing additional recipes—some inspired by famous bistros found outside France in places like London and New York City.

Turning our collection of recipes into a book was a group effort. We both want to thank Dr. Tim Ryan for his support, Tom Peer for encouraging us to take on the project, and a host of students and teaching assistants, especially Maureen (Molly) Brandt and Barry Graham, and others too numerous to mention who participated in recipe testing and photo shoots. You know who you are, and we are grateful.

Foods cooked and served with passion in favor of artifice have an elemental attraction. Whether a simple dish of field greens, a tender omelet filled with foraged mushrooms, or a dense and complex braise of lamb shanks, the foods and drinks that taste like they come from their own place are the fabric holding any great cuisine together. We hope you enjoy cooking and eating this food as much as we do. This is French comfort food, and you deserve some comfort, *à la française. A votre santé!*

Thanks to my brother, Tom, for making French food when we were young, my sister, Mary, for not throwing it at me, and my mother for being a great all-around cook who always made sure that everything on the plate tasted good together. Thanks also to my wife, Nathalie, who almost got tired of bacon.

– JOHN W. FISCHER

I have come to realize after 37 years in this profession that it is the people you meet along the way who make the difference in your life. They have the power to change your life forever. I would like to thank Brian Jones, Paul Gayler, Brian Turner, and John Miller for guiding, investing, and believing in me.

– LOU JONES

CHAPTER ONE

BISTROS AND BRASSERIES

The Pleasures of Casual French Dining

THE FOOD WORLD is chock-full of everyday terms that have vexing etymologies. The word *bistro* is said to be of Russian origin, because the Russian soldiers in Paris after the Napoleonic Wars would tell the French to move quickly, using a word that sounded an awful lot like a word for casual French restaurants. Other stories exist, but none seems to point out the true origin of the term *bistro*. The word *bistro* did not appear in print until the late 1800s.

What is important, though, is that we all have an innate sense of what a bistro is supposed to be—unpretentious, uncomplicated, casual, comfortable, and relatively affordable. Because bistros are a particularly popular style of restaurant these days, the word has been, perhaps, overused; there are so-called "bistros" serving everything from pizza to egg fu yung. For some of us, though, it's not a true bistro unless you can get a steak with French fries, a frisée salad with bacon and a poached egg, or French onion soup *gratinée*.

The term *brasserie* is a little bit easier to explain. Brasserie is the Middle French word for brewery, and usually refers to a casual restaurant that tends to serve more beer than wine. With its borders on Germany and Belgium, France has some regional cuisines that pair beautifully with beer. The beer-friendly dishes of those cuisines make up the bulk of brasserie menus—*choucroute garnis*, steamed mussels with fries, and *carbonnade*, a beef stew made with beer. Luckily for Parisians, many refugees from Alsace moved to the French capital (because of tussles with Germany) where they opened up restaurants. Sometimes, a Frenchman (or woman) just wants *une bière!*

Before we launch into our armchair journey of meals and memories we've acquired from our favorite bistros and brasseries, we wanted to examine the two key components in the French paradox: wine and cheese. Without them, would the French be truly French?

French Wines

IN EUROPE, PEOPLE DRINK WINE as a daily beverage. I don't abide by the phrase "wine is food," merely because wine is obviously a beverage. It is, however, served with almost every meal save breakfast. The sheer ubiquity of wine in France rivals that of soft drinks, iced tea, and milk on American tables. That's just it, though. Wine is as casual a beverage for the French and Italians as a soda pop or bottled iced tea is for most Americans. This is why there is so much importance in, and little attention given to, cheap wine in those countries. Everyday wine is an affordable everyday thing in Europe. It's what they have on hand, it doesn't beg contemplation…it's what they drink with dinner!

Most Americans who drink wine with a weeknight dinner will choose something that would be considered a bit special by many Europeans. The Côtes du Rhône that Americans might have with a burger might be something that a Parisian would save for Sunday dinner with the family.

Now, *vin de table* (table wine) is very low on the pecking order of French wine, but can still be pretty tasty and affordable. The category of *vin de pays* (country wine) has been good for the French in a number of ways. It has elevated the level of wine making while allowing some more latitude with grapes used and vinification methods. So, better-tasting, inexpensive wine is now available in volume, especially from the Languedoc region of France. So, if you see the words *Vin de pays d'Oc* on a bottle of French wine, chances are that it will be tasty, affordable, and pretty darned good for many of the dishes in this book.

French Cheeses

France loves cheese. There are cheese *laws* in France, and cheese is taken very seriously. There are approximately forty cheeses in France that have appellations, just like the laws that govern wine production. Tie in the various histories of some of these chunks of old dairy and you have a pretty complex subject to deal with. Let's break down the discussion of cheese into digestible tidbits.

MILK

The source of the milk used to make the cheese is the main ingredient, and has a lot of say in what the final cheese will taste like.

- COW'S MILK: *This is the most popular milk for cheese, partly because cows are big and make a lot of milk. If the milk is unpasteurized, it has an ivory color and quite a bit more flavor than pasteurized milk. Cheeses made from unpasteurized milk can only be imported to the United States if they've been aged for a minimum of sixty days.*

- SHEEP'S MILK: *This milk has about 75 percent more protein than cow's milk, and thus yields cheese with a different texture and flavor. Sheep do well in mountainous areas, and are often preferred by more rural farmers because of their relatively low maintenance (at least compared to cows). There are some very famous and delicious sheep's milk cheeses from the Pyrenees, including Bleu de Basques and Ossau Iraty.*

- GOAT'S MILK: *It's easy to find goat cheese on menus these days—in ravioli, on salads, and even in some desserts. The characteristic tanginess of this cheese pairs perfectly with some sweeter components, like beets, and strangely enough, helps the cheese to marry with some high-acid wines. For example, Crottin de Chavignol, a cheese that comes from a town right near Sancerre, goes remarkably well with wine from the same town. Somehow, the acidity of the cheese and the Sancerre cancel each other out rather than compound the flavors.*

RINDS

Rinds happen. The first ones that showed up were on cheeses that sat around for a long time without becoming inedible. Somehow, a tough exterior was allowed to form which protected the cheese from vermin while keeping moisture inside. This is a natural rind. Other rinds occurred over time, and are still in use on many cheeses. As you might expect, there are even laws to be found determining which rind should be on certain cheeses. I love the French!

- FRESH CHEESE: *As you might guess, there's no rind on fresh cheeses, such as fresh mozzarella, farmer's cheese, Neufchâtel, etc.*

This stuff is supposed to be eaten quickly and should never have the time to form any sort of rind.

- NATURAL RIND: *This rind just happens as the cheese ages and dries out on the shelf. The best example is Parmigiano-Reggiano; the tough exterior on this cheese is basically the same stuff as on the inside, it's just that the cheese aged for a year and the rind got tough and leathery.*

- BLOOMY RIND: *This is a specific strain of mold that is encouraged to grow on the surface of the cheese. The strain of mold is often a type of penicillum mold, such as* Penicillum camemberti *(guess from which cheese), and forms the white fuzzy coating, most famously seen on the surface of Brie and Camembert. It is, indeed, edible, and adds both textural interest and flavor complexity.*

- WASHED RIND: *This type of rind is feared by many, because this is often a sign that the cheese is going to be stinky. The way it works is that the surface of the cheese is washed with a salt brine, beer, wine, or marc (French pomace brandy, like grappa, and pronounced "mahr" in French), then allowed to dry out and age, or sometimes washed repeatedly, which results in a stronger flavor. The washing kills surface bacteria, allowing the desired strain of bacteria to grow on the surface of the cheese and form a coating. These rinds are often orange or pinkish in color, and have a distinctive odor. Okay, let's face it; these bacteria produce a putrid odor, like stinky feet or armpits. Cheese with a washed rind (luckily) tastes better than it smells. Famous examples are Taleggio, Epoisses, Pont l'Evecque, and Reblochon. It's usually a "yea" or "nay" proposition, you either love it or hate it. You will know quickly which camp you are in once you've tried any of these cheeses.*

- ARTIFICIAL RIND: *This refers to anything that didn't originate on that cheese, like the red wax on the Gouda or the dried herbs on the goat cheese log. There are even some cheeses that are wrapped in leaves (Banon is wrapped in chestnut leaves), or covered with the mold from another cheese altogether. In all of these examples, the artificial mold or covering protects the cheese from intruders and keeps the cheese moist.*

BUYING CHEESE

You should always buy cheese from a reputable cheese monger. These days, every major city and most large towns have a good cheese store. You want a store to have a good selection, fresh products, and a knowledgeable, friendly, and generous staff. You'll know it when you see it—and smell it!

Unless you have a dedicated cheese refrigerator, buy the smallest amounts possible so you won't keep cheeses longer than optimal. Also, tell the clerk what you like, and allow him or her to make suggestions as to what else you might enjoy. Don't just get stuck in a Morbier rut.

STORING CHEESE

If you didn't take our advice about buying small quantities, just remember that normal refrigeration is much too cold and dry for most cheeses. For temporary storage, wrap cheeses in parchment paper, butcher paper, or waxed paper, and keep at cool room temperature. Wet cheeses can be wrapped in cheesecloth, but should be stored under refrigeration. If you use plastic wrap, don't wrap your cheese too tightly—artisanal cheeses are living, breathing things, and you don't want to suffocate them. Dead cheeses can get nasty pretty quickly.

SERVING CHEESE

Always allow cheeses to get up to at least 60°F before serving them. You won't be able to enjoy the texture or complexity of flavor if you serve them at the normal American refrigerator temperature of 38°F. Some cheeses have traditional accompaniments, like quince paste for Manchego, but always serve cheese with some sliced bread or crackers. Olives can be a nice addition for a pre-dinner platter. Grapes are also nice to serve with cheese because they are sweet and refreshing. However, if it's a true cheese course you want (between main courses and dessert), go with just the cheese, bread and crackers, and perhaps a glass of dessert wine.

Beverages for Cheese

What a segue! Many of us have an innate belief that wine and cheese were made for each other. Not to disavow you of that belief, but dry wines can often clash with rich cheeses, and red wine is more often the culprit than white! Here, though, are a few simple ground rules for serving wine with cheese:

- SWEETER IS SAFER: Dessert wines are much easier to match with cheese than bone-dry examples. One of the best uses of dessert wine, which often doesn't go well with dessert, is serving it with cheese! Remember also that most famous blue cheeses have an equally famous sweet-wine counterpart, like Sauternes with Roquefort.

- WHITER MEANS LIGHTER: Whiter cheeses are younger and less intense than darker cheeses that have aged longer. Cheeses that are lighter in color have more water, less body, and tend to be delicate. Serve a more delicate, lighter wine with them.

- GROWS TOGETHER, GOES TOGETHER: This motto is especially true for old-world cheeses. Don't forget that there is often a wine produced in the same region as the cheese, so try them together! This category encompasses both the Roquefort with Sauternes and the Crottin de Chavignol with Sancerre discussed earlier.

Don't forget that beer can be a slam dunk with some cheeses, especially those from regions that are more beer-centric. For example, the Trappist monks who produce Chimay beer in Belgium also make cheese. Makes sense to us!

Whatever you do, be adventurous, try new cheeses, and never forget that one of the most impressive things you can do for your guests is to give them a great cheese course—it will be the easiest part of your entertaining, as unwrapping the cheese is the most difficult preparation technique required.

APERITIFS

If you have been to France, you know that the bars there bear little resemblance to American watering holes. Over there, when you go into a bar for something to drink, you'll most likely be enjoying coffee, water, or what the French drink before dinner–an aperitif.

Since aperitifs precede dinner, there are a few prerequisites: the drink has to taste good by itself, without food; it should never interfere with the flavors of the food to come; and a touch of acidity is considered *de rigeur*.

The aperitif served most often in this country is a glass of white wine. The most common aperitif in the parts of France we visited was a glass of Champagne or a Crémant from some other region. Of course, you can add Crème de Cassis, orange juice, or a sugar cube dowsed with bitters to a glass of bubbly to make a champagne cocktail, but that's only necessary if you get tired of Champagne. I never do!

Aromatized wines, including vermouth, Lillet, and Dubonnet, are cocktails in a bottle. Pour them over ice (or just serve chilled) with a lemon twist or slice of orange, and you have an aperitif!

The French prefer dry vermouth, the Italians sweet; and both were developed in the 18th Century. If you want a bit more excitement, a Vermouth Cassis is dry vermouth with a splash of Crème de Cassis served on the rocks with a lemon twist. Lovely.

Lillet is an aperitif wine fortified with fruit brandy, produced in the Bordeaux region by the same family that owns Château Ducru-Beaucaillou, a prestigious Bordelaise house. Dubonnet Rouge has the notable addition of quinine, which gives tonic its bitterness.

Two classic bitters, Campari and Cynar, both come from Italy and are relatively high-alcohol extracts of spices, herbs, roots, and other plant material. Some, like Campari, can be served as is, on the rocks, or with a twist. Cynar is generally served as an aperitif after it is mixed with something like soda, orange juice or tonic water.

If you ever stroll past a Parisian bistro and see someone sitting at an outdoor table with a chartreuse-tinted beverage in hand, chances are it's a Pastis. It is always diluted with water, and usually gets some ice, but not as much as an American might add. The two most popular brands are Pernod and Ricard. Pernod is essentially a legalized version of Absinthe, in that it has no wormwood, and thus no thujone, which was assumed (somewhat incorrectly) by the French to have been the substance that was having a psychotropic effect on drinkers. It is a little stronger than Pernod and has a slightly different flavor profile.

As for why the French would drink something with such a strong flavor before dinner, and in so doing, violate many of their very own aperitif rules, they would probably say, *"buf, c'est Pastis!"*

CHAPTER TWO

HORS D'OEUVRE ET SOUPES

Appetizers & Soups

Frisée aux Lardons

Crispy Bacon Salad

If SLAB BACON is new to you, try it in this classic bistro salad and you'll wonder how you've gotten along without it. The lardons add smoky flavor and a satisfying, chewy texture.

SERVES 4

2 heads frisée lettuce

8 oz slab or thick-sliced bacon

Salt and pepper as needed

2 tsp light brown sugar

¼ cup white wine vinegar

1. Wash the lettuce thoroughly and pat it or shake it dry with a clean linen towel.

2. Cut the slab bacon into *lardons* (see below). Heat a medium-sized sauté pan and add the bacon. Cook over medium heat, stirring frequently to gain even color on the bacon.

3. Divide the frisée among 4 plates and season with salt and pepper. When the bacon is crisp and golden, take the pan off the heat and remove the bacon with a slotted spoon; sprinkle it over the lettuce.

4. Let the bacon fat cool for about a minute. In another pan on medium heat, reduce the sugar and vinegar by half until it's syrupy. This is called a *gastrique*. Pour the gastrique into the warm bacon fat and stir thoroughly to mix.

5. Season the gastrique dressing with salt and pepper and spoon it over the salad. Serve immediately.

Cutting slab bacon into lardons. Begin by cutting the bacon into several large strips, then cut them into smaller pieces as shown.

BEVERAGE: WHITE BURGUNDY

This classic salad is a great combination of salty, sweet, bitter, tangy and smoky. It is not shy on flavor, and can use a pretty powerful white wine counterpart, and some oak could complement the bacon. White Burgundy from the Beaune would do well. Don't like oak? Go with a white from the Rhône.

Salade Niçoise

Niçoise Salad

FOR PURISTS READING this, several French chefs, including Eric Ripert and François Payard, have gone on record as stating that a true Niçoise salad can only be made with canned tuna, packed in olive oil.

DRESSING

¼ cup white balsamic vinegar

¾ cup extra-virgin olive oil

2 cloves garlic, crushed

10 basil leaves, finely chopped

Salt and pepper as needed

½ cup extra-virgin olive oil

2 cloves garlic, chopped, divided use

1 tbsp fresh thyme leaves, divided use

5 plum tomatoes, blanched and peeled

1 fennel bulb

1 each yellow and red pepper

1¼ cups new potatoes or fingerlings

4 cups arugula

3 cups mesclun lettuce

12 radishes, quartered

1½ cups haricots verts, parcooked and halved

6 artichoke hearts, quartered

3 hard-boiled eggs, quartered

6 anchovy fillets, cured in vinaigrette

1 can (12 oz) tuna in oil, drained

¾ cup black niçoise olives

SERVES 6

1. Preheat the oven to 275°F. To make the dressing, place the vinegar in a bowl and gradually add the olive oil while whisking thoroughly to form an emulsion. Add the garlic, chopped basil, and seasoning.

2. Prepare the salad's components. Brush a baking sheet with olive oil. Sprinkle a little of the chopped garlic and thyme onto the baking sheet. Cut the tomatoes into eighths and remove the seeds to make "petals." Lay these tomato petals onto the baking sheet, brush with some of the olive oil, and sprinkle with a little more of the garlic and thyme. (You should have about half of the garlic and thyme still remaining to add to the fennel.)

3. Place this tray in the oven and cook until the tomatoes lose their rawness and yield slightly to the touch, 15 to 20 minutes. Remove them from the oven and set aside to cool.

4. Parcook the fennel in boiling salted water for 10 minutes. Remove it from the water with a slotted spoon. Cut the fennel in half vertically. Slice it thinly using a mandolin set at ¹⁄₁₆ inch thick. Lay these slices on a baking sheet in

(recipe continues on next page)

the same fashion as the tomatoes. Brush with the remaining olive oil and sprinkle with garlic and thyme. Cook them the same way you did the tomatoes. The fennel will take a little longer to soften fully—about 30 minutes. Remove the fennel from the oven and increase the oven temperature to 350°F.

5. Rub the red and yellow peppers with olive oil and bake them in the oven for about 40 minutes, or until soft to the touch. Remove them from the oven. Peel away the skin, remove the seeds and stems, and cut the peppers into 2-inch julienne.

6. Cook the potatoes in boiling salted water for about 20 minutes. When cooked, drain and cool slightly. Cut into ¼-inch dice and, while still warm, toss them in a bowl with seasoning and 3 tablespoons of the dressing.

7. Mix the arugula and mesclun together in a bowl with a little dressing and season to taste with salt and pepper. Now for the fun and creativity: Arrange the mixed lettuces on your chosen plates and design your salad using all its component parts. If you're stuck for ideas, just look at the photograph on page 14. Finish the plate with a little drizzle of the dressing.

◇◇◇◇

NOTE:

Roasting the tomatoes, fennel, and peppers gives this salad complexity. The roasted vegetables can be prepared a day or two ahead of time. You could also blanch the green beans, hard-cook the eggs, and prepare the artichokes ahead of time, too. But, for the best texture and flavor in your potatoes, cook them no more than an hour or so before you plan to eat.

BY THE SEA, BY THE SEA, BY THE BEAUTIFUL SEA...

TWO THINGS MIGHT SURPRISE YOU regarding wines from Provence. One is that almost all (about 70 percent) of them are pink. The other is that these pink wines are dry. Since red grapes dominate the land in warmer growing zones, there are not many white grapes grown around Nice. But the lighter, fish-dominated diet there, combined with the very warm climate means that locals are looking for refreshing (that is, chilled) crisp wines.

So, the salad will be great with a bottle of affordable, dry rosé from southern France. Whether it's from the Rhône, Provence or the Languedoc, it will complement the tomatoes and peppers, while standing up to the flavor of the tuna. Conveniently, even the best bottles will cost less than twenty dollars.

Poireaux Vinaigrette

Leeks in Vinaigrette

SERVES 4 TO 6 AS AN APPETIZER

4 to 6 whole leeks

½ cup White Wine Vinaigrette*

**For recipes and information about substitutions,
see Fonds de Cuisine, page 175.*

1. Trim the leeks by cutting off the dark green leaves and root ends. Split the leeks in half lengthwise. Wash the halves thoroughly (remember, the leek pushes up through the soil as it grows, so dirt and sand collect between the leaves).

2. Tie the leeks back together with butcher twine to help maintain their shape. Boil or steam the leeks for 10 to 12 minutes, until a paring knife can be easily inserted into the thickest part of the bulb.

3. Place the cooked leeks in a nonreactive dish and pour the vinaigrette over them; allow them to cool. As they do, the leeks will absorb some of the vinaigrette.

4. Serve the leeks either at room temperature or slightly chilled.

◇◇◇◇◇◇◇◇◇◇◇◇◇◇◇◇◇◇

BEVERAGE: MENETOU-SALON

This wine might not be the easiest to find, but this neighbor of Sancerre produces a lovely Sauvignon Blanc that will match the acidity of the vinaigrette as well as bridge with the onion flavor of the leeks. Also, Menetou-Salon usually offers a better value than its more famous neighbor does.

Chevre Fermier Pain

Breaded Goat Cheese

IT'S AMAZING HOW a disk of warm breaded goat cheese can change the character of a simple green salad. There should be just enough cheese to stimulate, not dull, the appetite.

SERVES 4 TO 6 AS AN APPETIZER

4 oz fresh goat cheese

½ cup canola oil for frying

All-purpose flour, for dredging

Egg wash of 1 egg blended with 1 tbsp milk

½ cup bread crumbs, fresh if pan-frying,
*   dry if broiling*

¼ lb mesclun greens

Salt and pepper as needed

¼ cup Sherry Vinaigrette*

*For recipes and information about substitutions, see Fonds de Cuisine, page 175.

1. Cut the goat cheese crosswise into ¾-inch disks—it's easy if you use a piece of plain dental floss to slice through the log. You'll need one disk for each person.

2. To pan-fry, heat about ¼ inch of oil in a medium pan over medium heat. Dredge the disks in flour and shake off excess, dip them in egg wash and then coat with fresh bread crumbs. Pan-fry until they're nice and golden, about 2 minutes. Remove them with a slotted spoon and drain on paper towels.

3. To broil, coat the disks in dry bread crumbs and broil until they're lightly browned on top, about 3 minutes. These are quite delicate and require gentle handling.

4. While the cheese is warming, season the greens with salt and pepper, and toss with the vinaigrette. Separate the greens onto chilled salad plates. Place one of the warmed cheese disks on top of each salad and serve.

◇◇◇◇◇◇

BEVERAGE:

Goat cheese has a famous vinous counterpart in Sancerre. With the added richness of breading and pan-frying, a little more weight in the wine will help. Let's go with Pouilly-Fume, the bigger wine from across the Loire.

BLANCHAILLE À LA DIABLE

Devilled Whitebait

—❦—

WHITEBAIT IS ABOUT the same size as the much-maligned anchovy. This whole family of fish is very versatile, and this particular species is particularly tasty. In the United States you'll probably only find it frozen, either sold in solid blocks of many little fish or as individual frozen fry. Whitebait can be eaten whole; no gutting is necessary. It has excellent flavor and a crispy texture when fried!

SERVES 4

1 qt peanut oil

1 lb whitebait

1 cup all-purpose flour

Salt and cayenne pepper as needed

1 lemon cut into 8 wedges

¼ cup butter

4 slices whole-wheat bread

1. Heat the oil in a large sauce pot to 360°F. *Note:* When all the oil is used the pan should be no more than one-third full.

2. Toss the whitebait in the flour; shake the fish well to remove the excess flour. Use a slotted spoon or spider to drop the fish into the oil. Fry it in 4-ounce batches until golden brown, about 3 to 4 minutes per batch. Remove the fish and drain on absorbent paper. Season with salt and cayenne to taste. Serve with the lemon wedges and buttered bread.

◇◇◇◇◇◇

BEVERAGE:

Something relatively light with bubbles will be best here, so either a simple Crémant de Bourgogne or a crisp lager from Alsace, like Kronenbourg.

Warm Gravlax and Potato Salad

FINGERLING POTATOES ARE small, usually two to four inches long and about an inch in diameter. There are many varieties such as the Rose Finn (slightly pink), the Russian Banana, the revered *La Ratte* potato of France, and the variety that first inspired this dish, the Mandal (almond) potato of Norway. Choose these varieties of potatoes as you would any type of potatoes—free of blemishes, with a dry, tight skin. If you boil them in their skins before peeling, they'll have more flavor.

SERVES 4 TO 6 AS AN APPETIZER

1 cup Sherry Vinaigrette*

1½ cups fingerling potatoes, boiled and peeled

8 oz gravlax trimmings (recipe follows)

½ cup Fried Shallot Rings (at right)

1 sprig dill

*For recipes and information about substitutions, see Fonds de Cuisine, page 175.

1. Heat the vinaigrette in a nonreactive 2-quart saucepan or sautoir on medium heat for 3 to 4 minutes. Do not let it boil!

2. Slice the potatoes lengthwise, ¼ inch thick, and add them to the saucepan. Heat gently for 2 minutes then add the gravlax pieces. Do not stir, just gently nudge them around. Allow the gravlax to heat through for about 2 more minutes. (Remember, it's a *warm* salad.)

3. Remove the potato slices from the pan with a slotted spoon or spatula, and arrange them in layers on 4 warmed salad plates. Remove the gravlax from the pan with a slotted spoon and arrange over the potatoes. Drizzle some warm vinaigrette over the fish and potatoes. Garnish each dish with fried shallots and dill leaves and serve.

◇◇◇◇◇◇◇◇◇◇◇◇

FRIED SHALLOT RINGS:

Peel and slice 2 large shallots into thin slices. Separate the slices into rings. Season the shallot rings lightly with a little salt and cayenne pepper, then dredge them in flour and shake off the excess. Add enough canola oil to a small saucepan to come to a depth of about 1 inch. Heat to 325°F. If you don't have a thermometer, you can test the temperature of the oil by adding 1 shallot ring. If the oil is hot enough, it will immediately bubble around the shallot. When the oil is hot, add the shallots and stir gently to separate the rings. Fry until golden, about 5 minutes. Blot briefly on paper towels.

◇◇◇◇◇◇◇◇◇◇◇◇◇◇◇◇◇◇◇◇◇◇

BEVERAGE: WITH AN APPETIZER, ST. VÉRAN; WITH A MAIN COURSE, CHÂTEAUNEUF-DU-PAPE BLANC

The richness of the cured salmon begs for a little richness in its vinous counterpart. If you're serving the dish as an appetizer, the wine shouldn't be too big, hence the pairing of a Chardonnay with fuller body and acidity from the southern part of Burgundy. If this dish is the main event, pair it with a deserving costar that will have lots of richness and complexity, but still a decent level of acid.

Gravlax

SERVE THIS WITH dill mustard sauce and some hearty brown bread with good butter.

SERVES 10

1 salmon fillet (3 to 3½ lb), skin on

¼ cup coarse sea salt

¼ cup sugar

2 tsp crushed black peppercorns

Zest of 1 lemon

5½ cups dill sprigs

1. Scale the salmon and cut off the tail section where it begins to taper. (You can skin and save this offcut to grill or sauté and serve as a light snack or lunch.) Cut across the remaining filet to form 2 equal halves.

2. Line a glass, stainless steel, or plastic container with plastic wrap and place 1 piece of the fillet in, skin side down. In a small bowl, mix the salt, sugar, pepper, and lemon zest together. Sprinkle half of this mixture over the salmon fillet in the container.

3. Roughly chop one bunch of dill along with the stems of a second bunch and dress this on top of the salmon. Reserve the remaining dill to dress the cured gravlax. Sprinkle the remaining seasoning mixture over the second half of the fillet, and then place it on top of the dill on the first fillet, skin side up, to form a sandwich.

4. Cover the salmon tightly with plastic wrap and refrigerate for 48 hours, turning the salmon every 12 hours. It's best to begin this process in the early morning or evening so you don't disturb your sleep!

5. After 48 hours, unwrap the gravlax and discard the chopped dill, washing the fillets under cold running water to remove all cure ingredients. Pat the fish dry with paper towels and lay them down on plastic wrap. Chop the reserved dill and dress the gravlax to give it a green coat. Wrap the finished gravlax and store it in the refrigerator. It will keep for 1 to 2 weeks, depending on its handling.

6. To serve, slice the gravlax as thinly as you would smoked salmon. The dill will give each slice its characteristic green edge.

Dill Mustard Sauce

THIS SAUCE IS a classic accompaniment to gravlax but will go well with any smoked fish

MAKES 1 PINT

1½ cups mayonnaise

⅓ cup Dijon mustard

6¼ cups dill, picked and chopped

¼ cup whole-grain mustard

3 tbsp dark brown sugar

3 tbsp red wine vinegar

1 tsp lemon juice

Salt and pepper as needed

Dash Tabasco

Dash Worcestershire sauce

Mix all of the ingredients in a bowl until well combined and serve.

Les Fruits de Mer

SHELLFISH: OYSTERS, GOOSENECK
BARNACLES, LANGOUSTINES

THERE IS A GREAT TRADITION of shellfish being served to, and consumed by, the French. Formal restaurants do, of course, use both raw and cooked shellfish in composed dishes. Home cooks often buy oysters and shuck them at home, or even on the tailgates of their cars (see the sidebar below).

Perhaps the best way to enjoy shellfish, though, is at a casual restaurant with a raw bar; it's nice to have someone else do the shucking (and dispose of the shells). Tiered platters filled with crushed ice, studded with raw oysters and clams, steamed shrimp, langoustines, and gooseneck barnacles arrive at the table—appropriate sauces alongside. Beer and dry, light white wine go equally well with the provender. It's fun.

The assortment of shellfish you select is up to your personal taste and that of the people you are feeding. Just remember not to buy any shellfish that is less than fresh just because you think it's *supposed* to be on the platter. Also, don't avoid an item you are unfamiliar

---

TAILGATING ON OUR *TOUR DE FRANCE GASTRONOMIQUE*

WHEN WE WERE on our *Tour de France Gastronomique,* New Year's Eve was celebrated at the home of Chef Xavier LeRoux's brother. This being in Brittany, the meal began with a mind-boggling array of chilled shellfish served on ice. The serving vessels (literally) were miniature Styrofoam rowboats with Blavez Mad (Breton Gaelic for "Happy New Year") emblazoned across their bows. The meal was amazing, with the duck main course being served at 2 o'clock in the morning. Obviously, New Year's Day began a bit late for us, as we headed back towards Paris. We stopped to look at the Port de Bélon along the river of the same name. We hadn't seen Lou for a few minutes, until I spotted him through the viewfinder of the video camera I was using to document our trip. He was sipping Champagne and eating oysters with some locals who were picnicking from their car! He motioned us over, where we joined in the largesse of our mobile hosts. Under blue skies, bracing New Year's Day winds, enjoying good Champagne and Bélon oysters at the Bélon River was a good way to start the year.

with because of fear or prejudice—it might be the freshest thing in the whole store. Just ask the fishmonger how to prepare it, or follow some of the tips below.

OYSTERS

Few foods are as polarizing as oysters. Diners either passionately endorse the intake of these bivalves or are repulsed by them. Whether people compare eating oysters to either "kissing the ocean on the lips" or "eating salty boogers," you'll rarely hear someone say that they "can take 'em or leave 'em."

Edible oysters all belong to the family *Ostreidae,* and there are only a few different species that are commonly sold in the United States: *Crassostrea virginica* (including the Eastern oyster) *and Ostrea lurida* (including the Olympia oyster). The famous Bélon oyster is *Ostrea angasi,* and is also known as the European flat oyster. It may surprise some of you that all edible oysters fall into just two genera, especially if you've been to a raw bar where they had twenty different kinds of oysters available. The trick is that, somewhat like wine grapes, oysters are sensitive to their growing conditions. Different foods, temperatures, and even the shape of the estuary floor can drastically affect the shape, flavor, and texture of the oysters. This is why (as in wine) many oysters are named for their place of origin, like Nantuckets, Chincoteagues, and Fanny Bays—all of which are the same species.

The different species do, indeed, have some basic differences that might help you to pick a favorite. Bélons are wide, flat, and meaty, and great to cook with. Olympias and other West Coast oysters can often have a scent of watermelon rind and are rather soft in texture. We think East Coast oysters provide a good balance of texture and flavor, either raw or cooked. Try them all to see which you like best.

Once you've chosen which oysters you are going to serve, you need a stiff scrub brush, an oyster knife, and either a kitchen towel or a shucking glove. Scrub the oysters under running water to clean off mud and debris. Then, either hold the oyster in the middle of a folded towel on a cutting board or in your hand with the shucking glove. Make sure the flat shell is on top, the cupped shell on the bottom. Insert the oyster knife in the hinge (pointy part) of the shell. Wiggle the knife around, pull it out and wipe off the muck, then put the knife back in. When the knife feels like it is firmly in place, twist the knife to break open the hinge (this requires more technique than brawn.) Keep the knife parallel to and against the top shelf and sweep the blade forward to sever the abductor muscle from the top shell. Now, if you're French, you serve the oyster like this, with the bottom of the muscle still attached. I prefer to slurp the oyster out of the shell, so the muscle needs to be severed. To do this, turn the curved side of the knife down, and then gently turn over the oyster to present the rounded side on top. The oyster will appear plumper.

Whichever way you shuck the oyster, be careful not to lose any of the "liquor" that's in the shell—it tastes good. If the oysters are pristine, all they really need is a squeeze of lemon juice, and maybe a grind of black pepper. While folks like mignonette (a vinegar-and-cracked pepper sauce), hot sauce, or cocktail sauces, we say avoid the sweet, thick cocktail sauce because it obscures the flavor of the oyster. With all this talk of raw oysters, don't forget that fried oysters are fantastic, and can make a pretty good oyster po'boy sandwich. Ah, New Orleans!

CLAMS

These bivalves are not as popular in France as they are here in the States, but they are loved by many Americans, and thus belong on a shellfish platter on this side of the pond. There a few different species of clam available—the hardshell clam is the one most often eaten raw and in clam chowders. Quahogs, cherrystones, and littlenecks are readily available, and the last two belong on our platter. Littlenecks are the smaller of the two, and tend to be a bit more tender; Quahogs (pronounced *KO-hawgs*) go into chowder.

To open clams, you need a stiff scrub brush, a shucking glove, and a clam knife, which is slimmer than an oyster knife. Because clams are smoother than oysters and not as treacherous to open, holding them in your hand is safe and actually preferable because of the added grip of your fingers can offer. Scrub the clams under running water. Hold the clam with its front opening in the palm of your hand. Place the knife on the back of the clam and wiggle it into the hinge. Once in, twist the knife to pop open the hinge, and then take the knife out. From the front of the clam, run the knife up over the meat, against the shell to cut the two abductor muscles attached to it, then run the knife under the meat to cut the muscles from the bottom shell. Since clams have a stronger flavor than oysters, they can more easily handle the stronger flavor of cocktail sauce, but you can stick to lemon juice and hot sauce if you're a purist.

GOOSENECK BARNACLES

There are different kinds of barnacles. Some cling to dock pilings, ship bottoms, and rocks, and look like miniature albino volcanoes. Some barnacles, however, have a gray, leathery neck, and attach themselves to the same things that the other barnacles grow on. These "gooseneck" barnacles (called *percebes* in Spain and Portugal) are the ones worth eating. Considered a delicacy in Europe, they grow in Iberian waters, as well as off the coast of California. While decidedly unattractive, they yield a sweet flesh that is often compared to crab, lobster, and shrimp. The edible flesh lies within the neck, and goes well with other sauces that go with shellfish. The barnacles do need to be cooked, preferably by steaming, boiling, or quick grilling—but they will toughen if overcooked. Once cooked, the leathery neck skin should be split open, revealing the sweet flesh. In medieval times it was thought that these barnacles were the precursor to geese, partly because of their feathery appendages and long necks, and also because geese were never seen to procreate in Europe—they are migratory birds and spawned elsewhere. Luckily, if you eat a few of these barnacles, you will not be reducing the future goose population.

LANGOUSTINES

We had the chance to enjoy langoustines while in Brittany, where we celebrated New Year's Eve at the home of our colleague's brother. You can find articles detailing the vagaries of how langoustines are named. Known as Dublin Bay prawns or scampi in some parts of the world, a true langoustine is more closely related to clawless spiny lobster than it is to the shrimp that are evoked by the terms "prawn" and "scampi." That night, the langoustines had been lightly poached and were served with homemade mayonnaise on the side. Because langoustines, shrimp, and other crustaceans degrade in quality very quickly once they've left the water, it's not always practical (or affordable) to serve the more costly langoustines in the United States. If you are lucky enough to score some fresh, never-frozen shrimp (or, even better, langoustines), steam or poach them in their shells until *just done,* and then serve them with some good mayonnaise and lemon wedges alongside the other shellfish.

Plateau de Fruits de Mer

Seafood Platter

TO TRULY SERVE shellfish the way they would in Brittany, you would need some Styrofoam row-boats. Since you probably won't be able to find them, round platters of different sizes will suffice, with shellfish stands to support the upper platters, a lot of crushed ice, and, if you're really into it, some seaweed. Provide lemons, mayonnaise, sauce mignonette (a mixture of red wine vinegar, minced shallot, and cracked black peppercorns), and some wheat or dark bread with salted butter to accompany everything. Then, the shellfish for each person would be:

5 to 7 oysters of various types

6 clams (littlenecks)

A handful of winkles (little snails), poached in a cayenne-scented broth

3 langoustines (or shrimp)

Stone crab or spider crab

Each person should have access to a bowl to dump spent shells into, as well as cloth napkins and lemons to wipe off their hands periodically. While this is often considered an appetizer, you can pretty easily make this shellfish collection the centerpiece of the meal, perhaps by following it with a soup and salad. It really is up to you—and what you think your guests will enjoy.

◇◇◇◇◇◇◇◇◇◇◇◇◇◇◇◇◇◇◇◇◇◇◇◇◇◇◇◇

BEVERAGE: MUSCADET SUR LIE, SÈVRE-ET-MAINE, OR LAGER BEER

Perhaps the driest and simplest of all white wines, Muscadet stands in for the lemon that many a Breton would squeeze onto their oysters and shellfish. A crisp, dry lager beer will do just fine as an alternative to wine. If it's just oysters you're serving, Guinness Stout is a surprisingly perfect partner.

Blue Ribbon Brasserie

November 3, 1992, was a big day for food lovers in New York City when a little restaurant opened on Sullivan Street in the (barely) pre-boom Manhattan neighborhood of SoHo. Eric and Bruce Bromberg were raised in New Jersey, but were trained and worked in Europe, as well as some of the great restaurants in New York City.

They opened a small restaurant with a wide-ranging menu—from matzo ball soup and foie gras terrine to roasted pigeon and pupu platters. They also included a raw bar that sits prominently in the front window, with the great shucker Alonso shaking lobsters at passersby, hoping to lure them in. The menu, with its combination of highbrow and comfort foods, was enough to draw a crowd of conventional diners, but the operating hours of 4:00 in the afternoon to 4:00 in the morning drew many of us from the restaurant business after we were done at our own places. Most chefs and maître d's eat "family meal" before dinner service, around 5:00 in the evening, and so are pretty hungry at midnight, or 1 or 2 o'clock in the morning when they leave work. Sometimes a dozen oysters or some marrowbones with braised oxtail were just what the doctor ordered as a restorative, or perhaps as preparation for further revelry. Either way, the kitchen never closes before 4 a.m., and the surroundings are much better than those of a 24-hour diner . . . ditto the hip crowd.

The successful first restaurant spawned a sushi bar up the street, a bakery with restaurant in Greenwich Village, and now an outpost in Brooklyn's Park Slope neighborhood. The menu is more than just French food, and wine is at least as important as beer there but in true brasserie/bistro tradition, the Brombergs' mission is to serve delicious food quickly in a casual, bustling and fun dining room. They succeed.

Blue Ribbon's
Sautéed Calamari

THIS RECIPE COMES directly from Eric Bromberg of the famed Blue Ribbon Brasserie in New York City. As is typical for the dishes that he and his brother, Bruce, have created, the ingredients are very simple but the technique is rather specific. If you want your calamari to taste like it does at their restaurants, you need to follow the steps precisely. The entire cooking process should take no longer than 90 seconds or you'll have a batch of garlicky rubber bands.

When buying calamari, smaller is better because they're less tough than larger squid. Choose calamari with clear eyes and an ocean-fresh fragrance—they should not smell like fish, nor should they be slimy. If you're not going to use them that day or the next, freeze them in a tightly sealed plastic bag.

SERVES 4 TO 6 AS AN APPETIZER

1 lb small whole calamari

4 cloves garlic, minced

2 tsp extra-virgin olive oil

1 tsp pure olive oil

1 tsp unsalted butter

2 tsp chopped flat-leaf parsley

½ tsp fine salt

½ tsp pepper

1. Clean the calamari by removing the beak from the head and the quill from the tube. Reserve the tentacles. Make a lengthwise slit in the tube, and remove the purple skin from the tube and side fins. Cut the tube and fins crosswise into ⅜-inch strips. Leave small tentacles intact; cut large ones in half lengthwise. Keep the prepared calamari cold until it's time to cook them.

2. Stir the minced garlic into the extra-virgin olive oil and keep it near the stove.

3. Heat a sauté pan over medium-high heat. Add the pure olive oil to coat the pan. When the oil is shimmering but not quite smoking, place the calamari on two-thirds of the pan and the garlic-in-oil on the other third. Cook until the garlic is fragrant, about 10 seconds, and then add the butter on top of the garlic and the parsley on top of the butter.

4. When the garlic is lightly browned, after about another 15 seconds, stir or toss the contents of the pan to combine them; season with salt and pepper. Divide the calamari into warmed individual bowls, pour the pan sauce over them and serve *hot!*

BEVERAGE: ALSACE PINOT BLANC

The sweetness of the squid and the power of the browned garlic in this dish can use a wine with a firm hand, but no oak. Alsace is the second-driest wine region in France (because the Vosges Mountains block the rain clouds), so the wines tend toward intensity of flavor and aroma.

MOULES MARINIÈRE

Mussels Mariner-Style

⊸⊶⊷⊸

THIS IS A POPULAR DISH that shows up in one form or another in a number of cuisines with a strong tradition of seafood offerings. No matter which presentation you choose (and we are sure you'll love the version we offer!) every one of them is best served with some crusty French bread on the side to sop up the juice (our favorite part). Depending on where the dish is being prepared, different herbs (either fresh or dried) are added. We think the strong, clean flavor of flat-leaf parsley lends a structural backbone to the rest of the flavors in the pot. For a main course, serve the mussels with *pommes frites* and mayonnaise on the side—the famed *moules et frites* of many a roadside stand in France. Oh, and pour out glasses of whatever remains of the dry white wine you cooked the mussels in. Or, if you finished the bottle while you were cooking, you might consider serving a bottle-conditioned blonde Belgian ale.

SERVES 6 TO 8 AS AN APPETIZER, 3 TO 4 AS A MAIN COURSE (IF SERVED WITH FRIES)

3 lb mussels

2 tbsp unsalted butter

¼ cup minced shallots

3 cloves garlic, minced

¼ cup chopped parsley

½ cup very dry white wine

Pepper as needed

1. Just before you are ready to cook the dish, wash the mussels under cold running water and remove the "beards," which are the fibrous connectors protruding from between the bivalves' shells.

2. Heat large pot over medium-high heat. (Be sure to use a pot (with a cover) that is large enough to easily hold all of the mussels; you'll want to give them at least one big stir during cooking.) Melt the butter in the pot and wait for the foam to subside. Add the shallots and garlic. Cook until they're fragrant and translucent, 2 to 4 minutes, stirring occasionally to prevent burning.

3. Add the parsley, give it one stir, turn the heat to high, and add the mussels to the pot. Stir the mussels once with a large wooden spoon, remove the pot from the flame and add the wine. Return the pot to the flame, cover, and reduce the heat to medium, shaking the pot occasionally.

4. After 4 minutes, check if any mussels have opened. If only a few have opened, cover the pot again and turn up the heat. If most of them are open, remove them to warmed

(recipe continues on next page)

bowls and cover the pot again to let the last few open. After 1 more minute, transfer the remaining open mussels to the bowls. (The unopened mussels are either dead or stubborn. If stubborn, the cook gets to eat them later after they've opened, but if they're dead toss them.)

5. Decant the cooking juices to remove the grit at the bottom of the pot. (To make this step easier, set the pot so that it is tilted enough to make the liquid settle on one side. After it sits for a minute or two, the grit will settle to the bottom of the pot. Pour the flavorful broth carefully out of the pot, but stop as soon as you see the grit starting to make its way close to the edge.) Season the sauce with pepper as needed, and pour it over the mussels. Serve immediately, making sure each person has a place to put their spent shells.

◇◇◇◇◇◇◇◇◇◇◇◇◇◇◇◇◇◇◇◇◇◇◇◇◇◇

BEVERAGE: BLONDE BELGIAN ALE

If you're having these mussels with fries as a main course, the natural choice of beverage is a great beer from Belgium, such as Delirium Tremens. To stay closer to home, try a Hennepin from Brewery Ommegang in Cooperstown, New York.

Cuisses de Grenouilles Sauté aux Champignons du Bois

Sautéed Frogs' Legs with Woodland Mushrooms

FOR THE MUSHROOMS in this dish, I recommend an assortment of chanterelles, hedgehogs, hen-of-the-woods, and oyster mushrooms.

SERVES 4

48 pairs frogs' legs, about 1½ to 2 lb

Salt and pepper as needed

½ cup all-purpose flour

1 cup unsalted butter, divided use

2½ cups diced assorted wild mushrooms, cleaned

1 tbsp finely minced garlic

1 tbsp truffle juice

1 tbsp finely chopped parsley

½ tsp lemon juice

1. Soak the frogs' legs in ice-cold water for 1 hour to whiten and plump them. Drain and pat them dry with a paper towel.

2. Season the frogs' legs with salt and pepper and dust them with flour; make sure to shake off all of the excess.

3. In a large, thick-bottomed sauté pan, heat ½ cup of the butter on medium-high heat until hot but not browned. Sauté the frogs' legs until golden brown, 2 to 3 minutes each side. Remove them from the pan, place on warm plate or dish, and set aside.

4. Add the remaining butter to the pan and heat until the butter just begins to brown. Add the mushrooms and garlic and sauté until the mushrooms are limp, about 4 minutes. Add the truffle juice and reduce for 3 to 4 minutes over high heat, or until the sauce reaches a light nappé consistency.

5. Take the pan off the heat and add the parsley and lemon juice. Season the sauce with salt and pepper and pour it over the frogs' legs. Serve immediately.

◇◇◇◇◇◇◇◇◇◇◇◇◇◇◇

BEVERAGE: VIOGNIER

There's a lot of butter here, but also garlic, mushrooms and the frog parts. Earthiness, acid and power will all be found in a Viognier from Provence, like the one from Domaine de Triennes.

Gros Escargots de Bourgogne

Fat Burgundian Snails in Garlic and Parsley Butter

SERVES 4

3 tbsp finely chopped shallots

3 garlic cloves, finely chopped

¾ cup Chablis

1¼ cups finely chopped curly parsley

1 cup unsalted butter

¼ cup roasted hazelnuts, skinned, and finely chopped (optional)

Salt and pepper as needed

1 tsp lemon juice

4 dozen snail shells

4 dozen canned snails, drained and dried

1. Preheat the oven to 350°F.

2. Place the shallots, garlic, and Chablis in a medium sauté pan on medium-high heat and boil for 5 to 8 minutes, or until it reaches a syrupy consistency. Be careful not to let it brown because it will be the wrong color and add the wrong flavor. Pour this reduction-infusion into a bowl and allow it to cool.

3. Add the parsley, butter, hazelnuts (if you are using them), salt, pepper, and lemon juice to the cooled reduction and mix thoroughly.

4. Place about a teaspoon of butter into each shell. Add a snail and enough additional butter to fill it. Smooth the butter off so it's level with the shell. (This step can be done earlier in the day and the snails refrigerated until needed.)

5. Arrange the snails on a snail dish and put in the preheated oven for approximately 20 minutes, or until the butter melts and sinks down into the shells. Keep a close eye on the butter and do not let it boil over.

6. Serve the snails immediately with fresh bread to mop up the delicious butter.

◇◇◇◇◇◇◇◇◇◇◇◇◇◇◇◇

BEVERAGE: POUILLY-FUISSÉ (OR POUILLY-VINZELLES)

This wine, often mispronounced known as "poolyfoosy" (and properly pronounced *POO-yee fwee-SAY*) is a Chardonnay from the Macon region of Burgundy. It's not as famous as it used to be and so presents a decent value. Even better than its affordability is the fact that it has enough body to meet the snails head-on.

Steak Tartare

Tartar-Style Beef Steak

ONE OF THE best dinners we had while traveling through Burgundy was in a small bistro in Beaune, called Le Gourmandin. Cold, highly seasoned, and luxuriously raw beef with crispy, hot fried potatoes is an inspired combination of textures and flavors that goes marvelously with a light, slightly chilled *cru* Beaujolais, or even better, Champagne.

As an appetizer, serve this dish with *gaufrettes* (waffle-style potato chips), spicy mustard, and cornichons alongside; for a main course serve it with *pommes frites* and a salad. The raw egg yolk is a traditional and delicious addition. For appetizers, you could use a quail's egg yolk, but for main courses use a chicken yolk. The yolks can be coddled, but not cooked through.

SERVES 6 TO 8 AS AN APPETIZER, 3 TO 4 AS A MAIN COURSE

1¾ lb ground sirloin or sirloin steak, all fat and sinew removed

3 tbsp minced shallots

2 tbsp chopped capers

3 tbsp chopped parsley

1 tbsp lemon juice

2 tsp Worcestershire sauce

½ tsp salt

Black pepper as needed

Hot sauce as needed

1 raw egg yolk per diner

2 tbsp spicy Dijon mustard

Cornichons for garnish

1. To chop the meat yourself, start with whole, trimmed steaks. Traditionally, you would chop the meat by hand using a chef's knife. However, you can also chop the meat in a food processor: Use the metal blade and pulse until you have a somewhat coarse final consistency, with pieces of

(recipe continues on next page)

meat no larger than the size of a pea. If you are using meat that is already ground, start with the next step. In either case, remove all fat and sinew from your ground meat. You should have about 1 pound of meat left.

2. Gently stir the next 8 ingredients into the meat. Do not overhandle or you'll end up with a pasty consistency.

3. For appetizers, separate the meat onto chilled salad plates and create a small well in the center of each pile. Gently place a raw egg yolk in each indentation. Serve the appetizer with a teaspoon of spicy mustard and cornichons on the side. For main courses, separate the meat onto chilled dinner plates, place a raw egg yolk in each indentation, and serve them with hot *Pommes Frites* (page 71) and small, dressed watercress salads.

◇◇

BEVERAGE: BOURGOGNE PASSETOUTGRAINS OR BEER

Usually an inexpensive (for Burgundy) blend of Gamay and Pinot Noir (the name means 'chuck all the grapes in'), it will nicely match the fresh, metallic meatiness of the raw beef. Or, you could just have a beer.

SAUMON TARTARE

Tartar-Style Salmon Steak

‒‒‒‒‒

SERVES 6

1 lb fresh salmon fillet

1 tbsp minced shallots

2 tbsp finely chopped capers

2 tbsp finely chopped gherkins

1 tsp chervil

¼ cup sour cream

½ cup mayonnaise

Salt and cayenne pepper as needed

6 quail eggs

1 cucumber, peeled and thinly sliced

6 sprigs of dill

1. Skin the salmon fillet and remove all the small pin bones with tweezers. You can also buy the fillet prepared or ask your fishmonger to do this for you. Finely dice the salmon and place it into a bowl along with the shallots, capers, gherkins, and chervil. In another bowl, combine the sour cream with the mayonnaise. Use half of this mixture to bind the salmon mixture. Season with salt and cayenne pepper and refrigerate.

2. Soft boil the quail eggs by dropping them into boiling water then taking the pan off the heat. Remove the eggs after 8 minutes and cool them in cold running water.

Peel the eggs and store them in paper towels to dry them.

3. Reserve 6 cucumber slices and use the rest to form a ring in the center of 6 chilled appetizer plates. Set a ring mold or pastry cutter, 2 inches wide by 1½ inches deep, in the center of one of the plates, leaving a ½-inch border of cucumber showing. Fill the mold with the salmon tartar, and press a slight depression into the top with the back of a teaspoon. Carefully lift the mold away. Repeat until you have six plates prepared.

4. Make a cut halfway across the 6 reserved slices of cucumber. Overlap the cut edges of the cucumber to form them into a cup.

5. Place 1 cucumber cup into the depression on the tartare, and fill with a quail's egg. Coat the quail's egg with some of the remaining mayonnaise and garnish with the dill sprig.

◇◇◇◇◇◇◇◇◇◇◇◇◇◇◇◇◇◇◇◇◇◇◇◇◇◇

BEVERAGE: CHAMPAGNE OR CRÉMANT DE BOURGOGNE/ALSACE/LOIRE

The silky richness of raw salmon begs a somewhat racy counterpart, and a high-acid bubbly wine is just that…and the wine can be used as an aperitif that can go straight to the dining table to be served with the tartare.

Pâté de Campagne

Country-Style Pâté

GIVE YOURSELF PLENTY of time with this recipe so the duck breast can cure properly and the finished pâté has time to "mature" before being served—ideally with grainy mustard and pickled vegetables.

SERVES 10

1 duck (about 4 lb)

FOR THE DUCK BREAST CURE:

4 cloves garlic, finely chopped

4 sprigs thyme

4 bay leaves, crushed

⅓ cup salt

2 tbsp sugar

¼ cup unsalted butter

2 cups shallots, chopped

2 cloves garlic, chopped

10 oz pork butt, cubed and chilled and chilled

1¼ lb pork fat, cubed

2 tsp salt

¼ tsp black pepper

8 juniper berries, finely chopped

1 tbsp of your favorite dried mixed herbs

½ tsp grated nutmeg

Zest and juice of 1 orange

2 tbsp brandy

2 eggs

13 slices smoked bacon

3 bay leaves for garnish

7 juniper berries

TWO DAYS BEFORE COOKING THE TERRINE, CURE THE DUCK BREASTS AND PREPARE THE DUCK STOCK:

1. Remove the legs and breasts from the duck. Remove the fat from the legs and discard. Trim the meat from the legs and reserve. Keep the leg bones for the stock. Cut the skin and most of the fat off the breasts, but leave a thin layer of fat about 1/16th of an inch thick.

2. Mix the cure ingredients together and sprinkle half of it into an airtight container large enough to hold the duck pieces. Lay the duck breasts on top of the cure and sprinkle the remaining cure over the breasts. Cover and refrigerate for 24 hours.

3. Make a stock from the duck carcass and leg bones using the recipe for Chicken Stock (page 181). Reduce 1 quart of the stock until it reaches a syrupy consistency *(glace de canard)* and reserve. (Freeze the remaining stock for later use, perhaps in the sauce for Canard à l'Orange on page 102!)

1. Melt the butter on low heat in a small sauté pan and sweat the shallots and garlic in until softened, about 5 minutes. Cool them down and reserve.

2. Cut the duck leg meat, pork butt, and pork fat into rough dice. Place the diced meats into a bowl and season them with salt, pepper, the chopped juniper berries, herbs, nutmeg, zest and juice of the orange. Add the reserved shallots and garlic.

3. Warm the *glace de canard* to a liquid and add the brandy. Pour this mixture onto the meat, mix well, and let it marinate for 24 hours in the refrigerator.

COOKING THE TERRINE:

1. Preheat the oven to 425°F. Wash all of the cure mixture from the duck breasts and pat them dry. Cut the breasts into ¼-inch dice, and set aside.

2. Grind the marinated meats and the fat through a meat grinder or in a food processor (to use the processor, add the meat and fat in batches and pulse the machine on and off until it's coarsely ground). Place this forcemeat in the freezer for 30 minutes to chill thoroughly.

3. Beat the eggs into the chilled forcemeat. Fold in the diced and cured duck breast. Sauté a little of the terrine mixture in a pan so you can check and adjust the seasoning as needed. It's best to overseason slightly because flavors are subdued when food is eaten cold.

4. Line a 3-pint terrine mold with the bacon; overlap the slices slightly and make sure they are flush with the top of the mold. Fill the terrine mold with the forcemeat and level the top. Garnish with the bay leaves and the remaining juniper berries. Place a lid on the terrine and cook for 1 hour, or until it reaches an internal temperature of 140°F.

COOLING AND SERVING THE TERRINE:

Remove the terrine from the oven. Place a light weight on top so the terrine will sink beneath the fat and meat juices while it's cooling. When it has cooled to room temperature, place it in the refrigerator to cool completely, and then remove the weight. The terrine will improve with age, and if the fat seal is unbroken it'll keep for up to 2 weeks in the refrigerator. To serve, cut into the terrine crosswise and lift the slices out.

◇◇◇◇◇◇◇◇◇◇◇◇◇◇◇◇◇◇◇◇◇◇◇◇

BEVERAGE: BEAUJOLAIS-VILLAGES OR CRU BEAUJOLAIS

A high-acid, fruity chilled red wine will both cut through the fat as well as balance the simple meat flavor in the country pâté.

Soupe à l'Oignon Gratinée

Onion Soup

ONIONS ALWAYS MAKE me think of Alsace-Lorraine. So, perhaps a Riesling from there will do the trick here, or a Crémant d'Alsace whose bubbles will help cut through the richness of the cheese and sweetness of the onions.

SERVES 6

6 tbsp unsalted butter	*8 cups cold Beef Stock (page 182)*
8½ cups sweet onions, thinly sliced	*Salt and pepper as needed*
4 garlic cloves, minced	*Cayenne pepper as needed*
2 tsp curry powder	*12 toasted baguette slices, ¼-inch thick*
1½ cups Chablis	*3 cups grated Gruyère cheese*
2 tbsp all-purpose flour	*1 tsp chopped parsley*

1. Preheat the oven to 450°F.

2. Heat the butter on medium heat in a large, thick-bottomed pan. Add the onions and sauté until they're softened and a light caramel color, 20 to 25 minutes.

3. Add the garlic and curry powder and continue to cook for another 2 minutes, until the spices release their oils and subsequent aroma. Add the Chablis and reduce until the wine is cooked dry, 18 to 20 minutes. Add the flour and cook for 2 more minutes.

4. Take the pan off the heat and pour in the cold stock, stirring thoroughly to distribute the flour throughout the soup. Return the pan to the heat and bring to a boil; reduce the heat to low and simmer for 30 minutes.

5. Season the soup as needed with salt, black pepper, and cayenne pepper. Ladle the soup into oven-safe bowls, and top with slices of toasted baguette covered with plenty of Gruyère. Place the soup into the oven or under a broiler and cook until it's golden brown and bubbly, about 10 minutes.

6. Sprinkle each bowl of soup with parsley and serve it immediately.

Soupe au Pistou

Provençal-Style Vegetable and Pasta Soup

WHILE SOUP IS traditionally served without wine, this one is more of a vegetable stew, and is served well by a chilled pink wine from Provence.

SERVES 6 TO 8

1¼ cups dried haricot beans (white or navy), soaked overnight

1⅓ cups peeled, small-dice acorn squash

1 cup fresh fava beans or frozen lima beans

1⅓ cups peeled, small-dice russet potatoes

1 cup small-dice onion

1 cup cleaned, small-dice leeks

1⅓ cups peeled, small-dice carrots

3 stalks celery, diced small

2 cups small-dice plum tomato, peeled and seeded

3 cups haricots verts cut into ¼-inch pieces

1 bouquet garni (page 179)

1 can (7 oz) flageolet beans or ½ cup dried flageolet, cooked until just soft

4½ cups small-dice zucchini

1 cup elbow macaroni

Salt and pepper as needed

PISTOU

5 garlic cloves

Coarse salt as needed

20 large basil leaves

3⅓ cups grated Parmesan

⅔ cup extra-virgin olive oil

1. Drain the soaked haricot beans. Place them in a large pot and cover them with 4 quarts of fresh, cold water. Bring to a boil, then reduce the heat and simmer for 40 minutes. The beans should be just soft but not breaking apart.

2. Add the squash, fava or lima beans, potatoes, onion, leeks, carrots, celery, tomato, haricots verts, and bouquet garni and simmer it all for 15 minutes. Add the flageolet beans, zucchini, and macaroni and cook for 15 more minutes.

3. When the pasta is cooked, remove the bouquet garni and season the soup with salt and pepper as needed.

4. To make the *pistou,* place the garlic either in a pestle, food processor, or a blender with a little coarse salt, and process until it's smooth. Add the basil leaves and work it until the mixture is soft.

5. Mix in half of the cheese, and while stirring or with the blender or food processor running, gradually add the extra-virgin olive oil to form an emulsion.

6. To serve, add 1 tablespoon of *pistou* to the bottom of each bowl and ladle in the soup. Stir it very carefully to incorporate the *pistou.*

7. Sprinkle some of the remaining Parmesan over the soup, and serve.

CHAPTER THREE

OMELETTES, CRÊPES, GALETTES ET QUICHES

Pancakes & Egg-Based Dishes

THIN PANCAKES MADE from an unleavened batter have been around for centuries. There are numerous pancake eating traditions throughout the world. And, they have a tradition that encourages everyone to use up their old flour, as well as the butter and eggs used to make the pancakes and to fry them, before they begin the observance of Lent when such delicacies were forbidden.

Some traditions support the claim that *galettes*, a specific type of pancake common in Brittany, are actually the original crêpe. According to legend the early crêpes were made from buckwheat because the land could not support wheat. These buckwheat crêpes are now referred to as galettes, and they are typically paired with savory fillings. Today, Bretons use the word *crêpe* for sweet versions made from wheat and some sugar.

Now, buckwheat is not wheat at all. It yields a dark brown, flavorful, and gluten-free flour. The absence of gluten makes it a bit tricky to work with because the galettes are somewhat fragile, but the flavor is worth it (and people with an intolerance or an allergy to wheat can eat them too!).

Omelettes have a venerable history also, though they were probably preceded in history by the easier-to-cook frittatas. The word has many historical variations, but originates from the Latin word *lamella,* which means "thin plate." A true French omelette is the shape of a big cigar, about two inches at its widest and tapered at the ends (not at all like the "omelet" you get in an American diner).

Many contraptions exist to help the home cook make omelettes, including gimmicky pans that fold over in the middle. All you really need is a pan of the right size with a good, slippery surface, nonstick or well-seasoned and lightly oiled. Beyond that, you need the right amount of heat, plenty of practice... and patience.

Crêpes, galettes, and omelettes are very popular quick food in France, and there are often restaurants devoted to one or the other. The United States has not been untouched by this trend. There have been many crêpe restaurants stateside, including a chain called The Magic Pan, and a place called La Crêpe in Manhattan, across from Lincoln Center. Almost all featured the fine alcoholic cider from Normandy, and some had waitresses who wore traditional costumes that made them

look like Sister Bertrill from *The Flying Nun*. Currently, their popularity is not as great, but they seem to be on the upswing.

Restaurants dedicated to omelettes have not achieved the widespread popularity of crêperies, at least there has never been a mall-based chain of them as far as we know. There was, however, a very famous omelette restaurant in New York City on 61st Street, catty-corner from the famous Aureole Restaurant of Charlie Palmer (who, by the by, is a graduate of The Culinary Institute of America). The omelette-centric restaurant was called Madame Romaine de Lyon, and they professed to the availability of over 300 types of omelettes. It had old-world charm, and lived up to its promise, but like many other bastions of French cuisine in our country, has since faded away.

Galettes

GALETTES ARE BREAKFAST, brunch, or lunch fare in Brittany. Traditionally an egg is cooked sunny-side up in the center of the pancake while it is still in the pan. The egg is then surrounded by ham, sausage, and cheese. The edges of the galette are folded in to form a square with the yolk of the egg showing in the middle. The super rich filling explains the very plain wrapper.

According to Breton culinary tradition, the first pancake, the one that usually turns out to be the least beautiful, should be fed to the chicken that gave the egg for the batter. It is a good omen if the chicken eats it.

SERVES 4 AS A MAIN COURSE*

1 cup water

2 cups buckwheat flour

2 large eggs

3 tbsp unsalted butter, melted

1 pinch salt

2 tbsp unsalted butter, melted

Fillings (see suggestions on pages 56–57)

*This recipe is very easy to adapt to serve as many or as few as you have gathered around the table.

1. Put the first 5 ingredients into a blender. Blend them at medium speed until they're combined and smooth. Don't worry too much about overmixing because buckwheat is largely free of gluten. Allow the batter to rest for at least 30 minutes. Refrigerate it if you want to wait longer.

2. Heat a sauté pan on low to medium-low heat. When hot, but not smoking, brush the surface with butter and use a ½-cup measure to add batter to the pan. Immediately tip the pan in a circular motion to coat the pan evenly (if the batter doesn't spread easily, add some water or milk).

3. As the galette cooks, the edges will dry and curl up a bit. When the top surface is no longer raw and has a leathery look, 1 to 1½ minutes, gently pick up the edge closest to you with both hands and flip it to cook the other side. When steam rises from the surface and the bottom is lightly browned, 30 to 60 seconds, remove it from the pan. Add your choice of savory filling (see *Filling Omelettes, Crêpes, and Galettes,* pages 56–57) and fold it like an envelope, then invert it onto the serving plate.

◇◇◇◇◇◇◇

BEVERAGE:

Since the fillings are so varied, it's hard to pin down one wine or beverage. However, if you're making Bretonne galettes, a hard cider from Normandy will go with most, especially ham and cheese. Also, just about any sparkling wine will do just fine.

Crêpes aux Épinards et Fromage

Spinach and Cheese Crêpes

SERVES 6

12 Crêpes*

6 tbsp unsalted butter

1½ lb spinach, washed and stemmed

1 cup Mornay Sauce*

Nutmeg as needed

 Salt and white pepper as needed

½ cup grated Gruyère cheese

1 tbsp chopped parsley

*For recipes and information about substitutions,
see Fonds de Cuisine, page 175.

1. Preheat the oven to 450°F or preheat the broiler.

2. In a large skillet, heat the butter and add the spinach. Sauté over high heat until the spinach is wilted, about 4 minutes. Pour the cooked spinach into a colander and push out the excess water with a wooden spoon. Place the spinach in a medium bowl and cover to keep it warm.

3. Pour four-fifths of the sauce onto the spinach and mix thoroughly. Season with nutmeg, salt, and pepper to taste. Spoon 4 tablespoons of the mixture onto each crêpe and roll them up into cigar shapes.

4. Place 2 crêpes per person into buttered gratin dishes. Smear the crêpes with a little of the remaining Mornay sauce and sprinkle with the grated cheese. Place the crêpes into the oven or under the broiler. Remove when they're golden brown and sprinkle with chopped parsley. Serve immediately.

◇◇◇◇◇◇◇◇◇◇◇◇◇◇

BEVERAGE: ST. VERAN

Other than the browning of the crepe, there isn't much other flavor there, so the filling is what we need to concentrate on. Spinach in Mornay sauce is pretty rich and a little earthy. Let's try a St. Véran, from the Macon region. The shrimp and asparagus version could use a wine with an herbal or green edge to compliment the asparagus (which is not wine's enemy). White wine from the Graves region of Bordeaux will do the trick.

Crêpes aux Crevettes et Pointes d'Asperges

Savory Shrimp and Asparagus Crêpes

SERVES 6

1¼ cups asparagus spears

½ cup finely minced shallot

2 tbsp white wine vinegar

1 cup dry white wine

3 pt Fish Stock*

2 cups heavy cream

1½ tbsp all-purpose flour

2 tbsp unsalted butter

2½ cups cooked shrimp, 70 count, peeled and deveined

Salt and white pepper as needed

12 Crêpes*

1 tbsp chopped chervil leaves

*For recipes and information about substitutions, see Fonds de Cuisine, page 175.

1. Cut off the bases of the asparagus and peel the stems lightly. Cook the asparagus spears in boiling, salted water until just tender, 4 to 5 minutes. Remove the asparagus with a slotted spoon and immediately place them in ice-cold water. When they've cooled, remove and cut them into 1-inch pieces and put them aside.

2. To make the white wine sauce, place the shallots and vinegar in a large skillet over moderate heat. Reduce the vinegar until it's completely evaporated, about 4 minutes. Be careful not to color or burn the shallots.

3. Add the white wine and reduce the liquid to about 1 tablespoon, about 15 minutes. Add the fish stock and reduce it by two-thirds, about 40 minutes. Add the cream and reduce the sauce by half, about 18 minutes.

4. Mix the flour and butter together in a small bowl until a soft, almost runny paste is formed (this is called beurre manié). Add a teaspoon of the beurre manié to the sauce and dissolve it using a whisk. Bring the sauce to a boil. It should thicken slightly. Continue adding and whisking in the rest of the beurre manié until the sauce reaches a light nappé (coating) consistency, about 3 minutes total.

5. Take the sauce off the heat and fold in three-quarters of both the peeled and deveined shrimp and asparagus; reserve the rest for garnish. Season to taste with salt and white pepper.

6. Fill each crêpe with ⅓ cup of the filling. Roll up each crêpe and place onto a buttered dish. Smear a little of the sauce over each pancake, garnish with some shrimp and asparagus, and sprinkle with chervil. Serve immediately.

OMELETTE

SERVES 4

12 large eggs

Salt and pepper as needed

¼ cup unsalted butter

Fresh herbs (optional)

Fillings (see suggestions on pages 56–57)

1. To make the omelette, break the eggs into a bowl and beat them with a fork or whisk to break them up. Season with salt and pepper or any other seasonings you prefer.

2. Heat 1 tablespoon of butter in an omelette pan on medium heat until it's hot, but do not let it brown. Pour in one-fourth of the omelette mixture. Cook it over a medium heat, stirring occasionally with a fork.

3. When only a small amount of raw omelette mix remains on the surface, remove the skillet from the heat.

4. To roll the omelette, run your fork around the edge of the pan to free the omelette from the edges of the pan. Lift the skillet by the handle to a 45-degree angle. Tap the handle gently to encourage the omelette to slide toward the edge of the pan, until it forms a slight bowl. Add the filling of your choice in this depression.

5. Continue to tilt the pan so that the top edge of the omelette rolls down toward the bowl and over the filling. Keep tilting the pan over the plate until the omelette rolls out onto the plate and forms a cigar shape. Sprinkle the omelette with any fresh herbs you wish. Make the remaining omelettes in the same manner.

◇◇◇◇◇◇◇◇◇

CHEF'S NOTE:

Some recipes recommend adding a little water to thin and thus lighten the texture of your cooked omelette. A quarter cup of water would work for this recipe; just beat it with the eggs.

◇◇◇◇◇◇◇

BEVERAGE:

Eggs are delicate and rich, but also a blank canvas. The wine that is best for an omelette depends on the filling—somewhat. It shouldn't overpower the egg flavor, but should bear some connection to the filling. You know how much we love Champagne, and how flexible it can be with food. Lighter fillings, go for a Blanc des Blancs or lighter style. For richer or meat fillings, grab a Blanc des Noirs, a Rose or one of the fuller-style sparkling wines from France. Hey, eggs are cheap; spend the money on the wine!

Filling Omelettes, Crêpes, and Galettes

Adding a filling to a pancake or omelette is a very Gallic approach to the practical matter of wringing the most they can from whatever they have at hand. Use whatever speaks to you. Sour cream and caviar are always nice, but a simple dollop of jam or a few shreds of cheese also satisfy the hungry epicurean.

You can add a filling to your omelette before you roll it, just at the point when you've started to slide the omelette out of the pan and it has formed a bowl.

Another way to present your omelette is to roll the omelette out of the pan and onto the plate, then cut it open to make a pocket for a filling. Or, you can use a combination of the two techniques.

To add a filling to the omelette after you've rolled it out of the pan, use a paring knife to slit the top open. Spoon in the filling of your choice.

To add a filling to a crêpe or galette right in the pan, treat it like an omelette that you want to roll around a filling. Instead of rolling it up, gather the edges together to make a beggar's purse or an open-face galette. (See the description of the galettes served for breakfast in Brittany on page 50 for inspiration.)

Another option is to take the crêpe or galette out of the pan and put it on a work surface. Spoon the filling across the widest part of the pancake. Wrap the filling by lifting one side of the crêpe or galette over the filling and roll to serve right away or to tuck into baking dishes or casseroles to cover with a sauce and bake until bubbly. Make sure you get the open seam face down on the plate to keep it from unrolling.

Choosing and Preparing Fillings

Some fillings (cheeses, fresh fruits, smoked meats or fish) can be room temperature when you add them to the dish. But, typically, the filling should be warm to keep the dish from cooling down before you get to enjoy it.

Keep in mind that galettes and crêpes are inherently drier and retain less heat than omelettes, so their fillings should be moist. If your filling is fairly dry, consider putting a sauce either right on the filling or add it as a topping. Instead of dry diced chicken, stir it into a bit of Mornay Sauce (see page 185) or spoon on a sauce, as suggested for the smoked fish omelette on the next page.

We've included recipes for some of our favorite filled crêpes and omelettes. If you have any Boulangère Potatoes (page 81) leftover, warm them to serve with these dishes—they make a delicious accompaniment and, with the addition of a simple salad, you have a perfect lunch or light supper.

A Quartet of Filled Omelettes

Farmer-Style Omelette

MAKES ENOUGH FILLING FOR 4 OMELETTES

5 slices (4 oz) bacon, diced

1⅓ cups chopped onion

Omelette (page 54)

6 tbsp croutons

Crisp the bacon in a skillet; remove and drain it on paper towels. Add the onion to the bacon fat and cook until soft, about 5 minutes. Remove the onion and drain on paper towels. Mix it all together. Prepare the omelettes as described on page 54. Use one-fourth of the bacon and onion mixture to fill each omelette. Garnish each omelette with croutons and serve.

Ham and Gruyère Omelette

MAKES ENOUGH FILLING FOR 4 OMELETTES

6 oz chopped ham

1½ cups Gruyère cheese

Omelette (page 54)

2 tsp chopped parsley

Mix together the ham and the cheese. Prepare the omelettes as directed on page 54. Use one-fourth of the ham and cheese mixture to fill each omelette. Garnish each omelette with chopped parsley and serve.

Smoked Fish Omelette

MAKES ENOUGH FILLING FOR 4 OMELETTES

10 oz smoked fish (salmon, haddock, or mackerel)

2 tsp Sauce Raifort*

Omelette (page 54)

Chopped chervil as needed, for garnish

*For recipes and information about substitutions, see Fonds de Cuisine, page 175.

Flake or cut the fish into small pieces. Prepare the omelettes as described on page 54. Use one-fourth of the smoked fish to fill each omelette and spoon on ½ tsp Sauce Raifort before rolling the omelette. Garnish with chervil and serve.

Mushroom and Chive Omelette

MAKES ENOUGH FILLING FOR 4 OMELETTES

½ cup minced shallots

2 tbsp unsalted butter

3 cups mushrooms, sliced

Omelette (page 54)

Chives as needed, for garnish

Sweat the shallots in butter for about 5 minutes, add the mushrooms, and reduce the juices until dry, another 5 to 10 minutes. Prepare the omelettes as described on page 54. Use one-fourth of the mushroom mixture to fill each omelette. Garnish each omelette with chives and serve.

Raclette

HALF DINNER, HALF GET-TOGETHER, this traditional cheese dish rivals fondue for popularity in its home territories of Switzerland and the northeast of France. From the French verb *racler,* "to scrape," raclette was originally made by shepherds who would take half a wheel of cheese and prop it in front of the campfire to melt. As the cheese softened, they would scrape it off the wheel and onto pieces of bread.

Today, there are two popular ways of preparing the dish. One involves a tool that holds half a wheel of raclette cheese right under a heat lamp. Much like the shepherds' version, the melted cheese is scraped off and served over boiled potatoes with pickled vegetables on the side. At home it's best to use a raclette grill. This device is like an electric griddle, but with space beneath the cooking surface for small individual pans.

The cheese goes onto the guest's pan (with fresh vegetables, if desired), under the grill, and is poured over the potatoes when it's melted. These grills are readily available—we've seen them in stores and online. Frankly, the process does result in a certain amount of *odeur* in the room, but one raclette web site suggests leaving an orange or lemon studded with cloves on the dining table overnight if you feel the need to eliminate the memory.

While both methods of making raclette are very simple, the more involved technique using the grill is described at right.

If you want to create conviviality at a dinner party, there's nothing like forcing your guests to make their own dinner. Of course, fondue was big in the 1970s, but raclette is easier to prepare and perhaps a bit more hip. Fondue, if done well, involves making a roux, whisking . . . actual cooking! Raclette involves mostly, well, melting. Sure, potatoes need to be boiled and maybe some vegetables prepared, but the use of the heat lamp or grill leaves most of the work to the appliance.

Raclette grills are very easy to find either online or in home goods stores, which makes us wonder, exactly how many Americans are making this dish on a regular basis? However many there are, we think that you should join their ranks.

To make a great raclette, be sure to check the label for the real thing. As soon as you've scraped off the first melted layer, heat the cheese again.

MAKES AS MANY SERVINGS AS YOU FEEL LIKE PREPARING

1½ cups small, waxy potatoes per person

6 to 7 oz raclette cheese per person

12 slices prosciutto or speck per person (optional)

Sliced raw vegetables, such as mushrooms, sweet peppers, tomatoes and onions (optional)

Sweet paprika as needed

Ground black pepper as needed

Cornichons as needed

Pickled onions as needed

1. Wash the potatoes, leaving the skins on, and boil in well-salted water for 20 to 30 minutes. When they're just done, drain them. Keep the potatoes warm for the duration of the meal by either returning them in the pot with a towel or piece of foil sandwiched between the pot and its lid, or placed in a warmed serving dish that can be covered to keep the potatoes warm.

2. Cut the cheese into slices about ½-inch thick, and just smaller than the grill's pans.

3. Give each guest access to the sliced cheese, meats, vegetables, and garnishes. Have each guest fill their pan with one slice of cheese and whatever vegetables they choose, then slide the pans under the grill.

4. Let the cheese get melted and bubbly, but not too hot because the protein and fat can separate. Pour the melted cheese over 1 or 2 boiled potatoes and eat with a couple of cornichons and pickled onions.

5. Before tucking into the melted cheese and potato conglomeration, set up the pan with fresh cheese and vegetables and put it under the grill so it'll be ready to eat when you finish eating the first batch.

◇◇◇◇◇◇◇

BEVERAGE:

The traditional beverage for raclette is hot tea, which is thought to aid digestion. Wine and beer are just fine, though, with our preference being dry white wine from Savoy or Alsace. Since the dish originated in Switzerland, a Swiss Chasselas-based white wine would be correct in a cultural sense, but is not always a good value or, for that matter, available. If you can find it, give it a shot; otherwise, Pinot Gris from Alsace or Chasselas from Savoy will get the job done.

Tarte Flamiche

Leek and Cheese Tart

BOTH SAVORY AND sweet custards benefit from the milk or cream (or both) being scalded prior to mixing with the eggs, egg yolks, or both. Pouring a warmed custard into the pastry shell will ensure quick, even cooking, preventing the tart from "souffléeing" around the edges while waiting for the center to cook. A few of my students have paraded their souffléd tarts, quiches, and similar custard-based dishes with great pride, blissfully unaware that they have ruined the custard. Instead of being sublimely smooth and silken, it will have a grainy texture. As upsetting as these occasions are for the student, they do make excellent teaching opportunities for us teachers.

MAKES ONE 9-INCH TART; SERVES 8

¾ lb Pâte Brisée,* blind-baked

2 tbsp unsalted butter

2 cups small-dice leeks

4 large eggs

1 large egg yolk

Salt and pepper as needed

1 cup milk

1 cup heavy cream

1 cup grated Gruyère cheese

⅓ cup chopped chives

*For recipes and information about substitutions, see Fonds de Cuisine, page 175.

1. Preheat the oven to 325°F. Melt 2 tablespoons of butter in a sauté pan and add the leeks. Sweat the leeks on medium heat until soft, about 5 minutes; set aside to cool.

2. Whisk together the eggs, egg yolk, salt, and pepper in a medium bowl. Scald the milk and the cream in a saucepan on medium-high heat and pour a little at a time onto the beaten eggs mixture. Pass the custard through a fine-mesh strainer into another bowl.

3. Layer the leeks and cheese into the blind-baked tart.

4. While the custard is still warm, pour as much of it as the tart will hold over the leeks and cheese, and carefully place the tart into the oven. Bake for 30 to 45 minutes or until the custard is set and has a golden color.

5. Remove the tart from the oven and allow it to cool for 10 minutes before cutting. Sprinkle with chives and serve with a crisp salad.

◇◇◇◇◇◇◇◇◇◇◇◇◇◇◇◇◇◇◇◇◇◇◇

BEVERAGE: ALSACE EDELZWICKER

Edelzwicker means "noble wine." This mixture of grapes usually produces a low-priced and tasty wine, especially if it comes from a well-known producer like Albert Boxler.

Quiche Lorraine

Onion and Bacon Quiche

ALTHOUGH *"REAL" MEN* supposedly don't eat quiche, they certainly make it. This dish comes from the Lorraine region near Alsace, an area famous for its dairy production. Some say that the onion in this dish turns it into a quiche Alsacienne. So be it. I just think it tastes good. While the Lorraine version is the most famous of this genre, many others exist, like the rapturous Tarte Flamiche on the preceding page.

SERVES 4 TO 6 AS A MAIN COURSE, 6 TO 8 AS AN APPETIZER

¾ lb Pâte Brisée,* blind-baked

5 slices smoked bacon

½ cup fine-dice yellow onion

1 cup heavy cream

4 large eggs

1 tsp salt

½ tsp ground white pepper

½ cup shredded Swiss-type cheese (preferably Gruyère)

*For recipes and information about substitutions, see Fonds de Cuisine, page 175.

1. Preheat the oven to 325°F.

2. Cook the bacon in a medium sauté pan on medium heat until crisp, and then drain it on paper towels, crumble, and reserve. Keep 1 teaspoon of the bacon fat in the pan. Sauté the onions in the bacon fat until tender, 6 to 8 minutes. Remove and allow them to cool to lukewarm.

3. Heat the cream over low heat until very hot (it isn't necessary to bring it to a full boil, but you should see plenty of steam rising from the surface, and probably some bubbles around the edges). Whisk the eggs in a medium bowl until they're blended; pour on the cream and whisk until the cream and eggs are blended. (Mix gently; the custard mixture should not be frothy.) Stir in salt and pepper.

4. Scatter the bacon, onions, and cheese evenly over the cooked pie shell. Pour the custard mixture over the contents of the pie shell.

5. Carefully place the quiche onto a baking sheet on the middle rack of the oven and cook it for 30 minutes, or until the center is barely set. A 2-inch circle in the center of the quiche (think of it as the bull's-eye) should wiggle when you jiggle the tart.

6. Remove the quiche from the oven and allow it to cool on a wire rack. Serve warm or at room temperature with a green salad.

◇◇◇◇◇◇◇◇◇◇◇◇◇◇◇◇◇◇◇◇◇◇◇◇

BEVERAGE: ALSACE GEWURZTRAMINER

Gewurztraminer can be too much for some food, but just stay away from the reserve and more expensive versions from Alsace, and they will have less intensity. So, Trimbach or Willm basic Gewurztraminer, or even one from New York, like the one from Lenz Vineyards on Long Island. Fresh and a little funky.

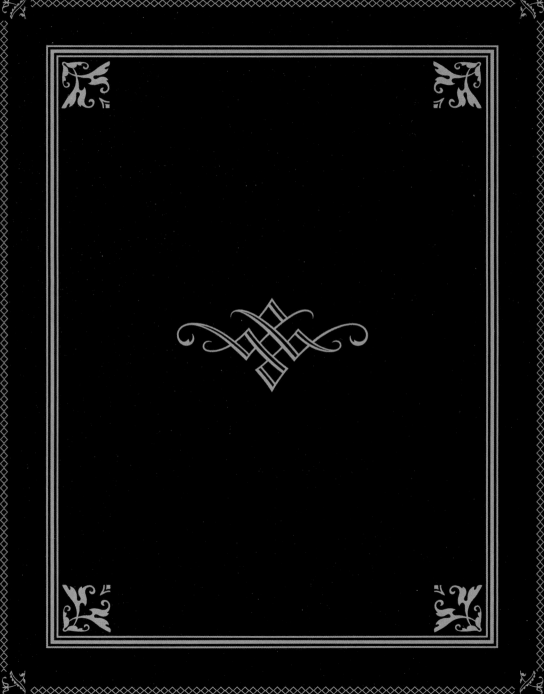

CHAPTER FOUR

ACCOMPAGNEMENTS

Side Dishes

Chou de Bruxelles aux Lardons

Brussels Sprouts with Bacon

WHILE SMALLER SPROUTS are more tender, you'll want to use ones that are large enough to cut in half—1 to 1½ inches in diameter is a good size. Choose Brussels sprouts that are bright-green, firm, and tightly packed. There should not be any give when squeezed, and their stem ends should not be dried out or brown.

SERVES 6 AS A SIDE DISH; RECIPE CAN BE DOUBLED (OR TRIPLED) AS NEEDED

1½ lb Brussels sprouts	¾ cup dry white wine
2 oz slab bacon	½ cup Chicken Stock*
1 tbsp olive oil	½ tsp salt
2 large shallots, minced	¼ tsp black pepper

*For recipes and information about substitutions, see Fonds de Cuisine, page 175.

1. Wash the sprouts and pull off any damaged or tough-looking leaves. Wipe them dry with a paper towel, cut them in half from bottom to top, and set aside.

2. Cut the bacon into lardons and render them in olive oil as directed on page 178.

3. Raise the heat to medium-high and add the shallots to the rendered bacon fat. When they're translucent, after about 2 minutes, add the sprouts to the pan. Make sure most of the pieces spend some time "face-down" so they will brown. After about 3 minutes, or when most of them have gotten some color, remove the pan from the heat to add the wine and return it to the heat so the liquid can reduce to about ½ cup. Lower the heat to medium-low, and then add the stock, salt, and pepper.

(recipe continues on next page)

Loving Brussels sprouts

We know that many of you have this member of the cabbage family at the top of your most-hated-foods list. It could be your mom's fault, or maybe Aunt Jeanette's—whoever cooked the cute cruciferous spheroids until they formed an odiferous paste. For those of you willing to give Brussels sprouts another chance, there are some common cooking strategies we use here, plus a new one.

The most common ploy to make members of the *Brassica* family attractive to collard and cabbage haters is to add some form of pork fat. Almost as common is to use a cooking method that will allow some caramelization to occur without overcooking them. Lastly, a bit of acidity (often cider vinegar) is usually added just before serving to balance the fat and sweetness of the dish.

Here is where we'll depart from the norm by using wine during the cooking rather than adding vinegar at the end. While you should usually avoid cooking green vegetables with an acid (if you want the vegetable to stay bright green), Brussels sprouts rarely retain their emerald hue anyway, and the subtlety of the acidity in this version is quite beguiling.

4. Cook the sprouts partially covered until they're tender, 20 to 25 minutes total cooking time. To check for doneness, stick the tip of a paring knife into the core of one of the larger sprout halves; you should feel moderate resistance. To check for deliciousness, eat one. These sprouts are superb when served with roasts, steaks, and even whole-roasted fish.

CÉLERI RÉMOULADE

Celery Root Salad

⸻⸺⸗⸺⸻

THIS POPULAR BISTRO SALAD is basically the French version of coleslaw. Celery root, also known as celeriac and celery knob, is a cultivar of the celery family that is grown for its turnip-sized root—the leaves and stalks are pretty much unusable. The lemon juice and salt used at the beginning of the recipe help to tenderize the celeriac, which is then dressed with the other ingredients.

SERVES 4 TO 6 AS A SIDE DISH

1 celery root (1½ to 2 lb)

2 tsp lemon juice

1 tsp salt

½ cup mayonnaise

2 tsp Dijon mustard

2 tsp grainy mustard

1 tsp white wine vinegar

Pepper as needed

1. Peel the celery root using a serrated knife or large chef's knife. Cut it into quarters and either julienne by hand or with a food processor's julienne or large-hole grating blade.

2. Toss the julienned celery root in a large nonreactive bowl with the lemon juice and salt. Allow it to sit at least 15 minutes to tenderize a bit.

3. Meanwhile, to make a dressing, whisk together the rest of the ingredients in a nonreactive bowl. Pour the dressing over the celery root and adjust seasoning with salt and pepper as needed. The final salad should be creamy and have a nice lemon-and-mustard contrast to the rich mayonnaise.

Oignons Farcies

Stuffed Onions

FOR A COMPLETE meal, serve these stuffed onions with mashed potatoes and a green vegetable with crisp bacon lardons. This is an old-fashioned dish that I remember from my training in the 1970s. Onions were a commonly braised vegetable then, along with celery, chicory (Belgian endive), and leeks. It was good to bring braised onions back to life through this book. I also decided to stuff the onions for a more substantial meal, although originally they would not have been stuffed.

SERVES 6

6 medium Spanish onions (6 to 8 oz each)

2 tbsp unsalted butter

1 garlic clove, crushed to a paste

1¾ cups cèpes, chanterelle, or cremini mushrooms, roughly chopped

¼ cup dry white wine

12 oz ground pork shoulder

1 tsp dried sage

Nutmeg as needed

2 tbsp chopped parsley, divided use

1 large egg

1 cup bread crumbs

Salt and pepper as needed

1 qt Demi-glace*

*For recipes and information about substitutions, see Fonds de Cuisine, page 175.

1. Preheat the oven to 325°F. Trim the root end of the onions, removing the roots but leaving the root end intact to hold it together as it braises. Peel the onions from the root up removing only the first layer of peel. This may leave some peel at the top from the second layer of the onion. Don't worry about it—your onions should have a nice point to their tops.

2. Blanch the onions in boiling salted water for 5 minutes. Refresh them in cold water until they're cooled. Cut off about 1 inch of the tops and reserve.

3. To prepare the onion to stuff, you must remove the inside. To do that, hold your paring knife horizontally so that you can insert the tip into the onion, piercing into it about ½ inch up from its base, and about ½ inch in from the outer edge. Cut across the onion (your cut should be parallel to your work surface) to within ½ inch of the other side. (See the photo illustrating this technique on the following page.) Be careful not to cut completely across the onion. Next, cut into the top of the onion holding the knife vertically so your knife blade can cut from the top of the onion and around the center of the onion. This cut should be about ¼ inch in from the edge. Cut all around the onion, and down to the

(recipe continues on next page)

horizontal cut. When you have completed the circle, you can "fish" the inside of the onion out with the tip of your knife.

4. To prepare the stuffing, heat the butter in a medium pan and sauté the garlic for 30 seconds over low heat. Add the mushrooms and continue to sauté for 2 minutes, or until they soften. Add the wine and reduce the liquid by half over medium heat. Remove the mix from the burner and allow it to cool.

5. Add the pork, sage, nutmeg, 1 tablespoon of the chopped parsley, egg, and bread crumbs and mix it all well; season with salt and pepper.

6. Stuff the onions with this mixture until they're full and cover them with their tops. Place them into a 2-inch deep roasting pan just big enough for the onions to fit snugly.

7. Bring the demi-glace to a boil and pour it over the onions. Liberally baste the onions with the demi-glace, and then bake the onions, uncovered, for 1½ hours, or until they're tender. Baste them frequently throughout the cooking.

8. When the onions are cooked, carefully remove them from the tray and onto a serving dish; keep them warm. Reduce the braising liquid over high heat until it coats the back of a spoon. Season the sauce with salt and pepper and spoon it over the onions. Sprinkle the onions with the remaining tablespoon of chopped parsley and serve.

After you have cut off the top slice, scored the onion around its base, and then cut down into the onion to free the inner layers, insert the tip of your knife into the inside portion of the onion. Use the knife as a lever to lift and pry out the center. You can save this piece to add to other dishes that call for minced or diced onion. Soupe à l'Oignon Gratinée (page 43) or Carbonnades à la Flamandes (page 143) are great options.

POMMES FRÎTES

French Fries

3½ lb russet potatoes

Canola or peanut oil as needed

Salt as needed

1. Peel the potatoes and cut them into ¼-inch by ¼-inch sticks (you can use a mandolin for this job). Hold the potatoes in cold water until you're ready to blanch. Just before blanching the fries, pat them dry with a clean linen or paper towel.

2. Add the oil to a deep fryer or a deep pot; there should be at least 2 or 3 inches of oil to fry the potatoes. Heat the oil to 300°F. (It's very important to observe the deep-frying safety rules on page 178.)

3. Blanch the potatoes in 2 batches. Maintain the oil temperature until the fries are cooked yet have no color, 3 to 4 minutes. Remove them from the oil with a slotted spoon and drain them on paper towels.

4. When you're ready to serve the fries, heat the oil to 360°F and cook them in 2 batches until they're crisp and golden, 3 to 5 minutes. Remove them with a slotted spoon, sprinkle with salt, and serve immediately.

◇◇◇◇

NOTE:

The word "blanch" literally means to whiten. To blanch the fries means cooking without coloring. This two-stage cooking method will ensure a crisp surface with a fluffy interior.

Ragout de Champignons

Mushroom Ragoût

THIS HIGHLY VERSATILE and very tasty basic preparation can be used as an accompaniment for almost any hearty main course. It is also delicious as a bed for grilled meats or fish, as a component in quiches or tarts, or even as a filling for galettes and omelettes. Depending on what it will be used for, different herbs can be used. For instance, to accompany roast chicken, tarragon would work nicely; for lamb, thyme. If you're not sure how the ragoût will be used, use either parsley or no herb at all. The dried mushrooms will add a ton of rich flavor no matter what kind of fresh mushrooms you use, even the good old white variety found in the supermarket. Feel free to use more exotic varieties such as oysters, shiitakes, chanterelles, hen-of-the-woods, or morels, but the dried mushrooms are the ones bringing most of the flavor to this dish.

SERVES 6 TO 8 AS A SIDE DISH

¾ oz (about 6) dried mushrooms (porcini or cèpes)

5 cups fresh mushrooms (porcini or cèpes)

3 tbsp unsalted butter

1 tbsp olive oil

2 large shallots, minced

2 garlic cloves, finely minced

1 cup dry white wine

½ tsp salt

¼ tsp black pepper

1 cup Chicken Stock*

*For recipes and information about substitutions, see Fonds de Cuisine, page 175.

1. Soak the dried mushrooms in very hot water (tap is okay, it doesn't have to be boiling) until reconstituted, 5 to 10 minutes. Drain the mushrooms and reserve the liquid. Chop them into ½-inch pieces and set aside.

2. Clean the fresh mushrooms, first trimming the stem end and then wiping them with a soft cloth or brush. (Try to avoid rinsing them in water unless you have mushrooms with tightly closed caps. If you must rinse mushrooms, get them out of the water as quickly as possible and dry them on a stack of paper toweling.) Cut large mushrooms into quarters, medium-size ones in half, and leave small ones whole.

2. Heat the butter over medium heat in a sauté pan large enough to hold all of the fresh mushrooms.

3. Raise the heat to high and add the fresh mushrooms. Do not stir until the cut edges are starting to brown, about 4 minutes. When the mushrooms have absorbed all of the butter but

(recipe continues on next page)

have not yet browned, about 2 minutes, add the olive oil. Add the shallots and cook until they're translucent, about 2 minutes. Add the garlic and cook until fragrant, 1 to 2 minutes. Stir or toss once or twice, lower to medium heat and add the reconstituted dried mushrooms.

4. When the fresh mushrooms are lightly browned, pour in the white wine and reduce until liquid just covers the bottom of the sauté pan, about 7 minutes. Add ¼ cup of the reserved reconstituted mushroom liquid and reduce it by half, about 4 minutes. Add the chicken stock and reduce until the liquid is the consistency of half-and-half, about 4 minutes. Season with salt and pepper. The ragoût is now ready and can be served immediately, or cooled slightly and served at room temperature. The ragoût can be refrigerated for up to a week or frozen for 6 months.

Tartiflette

Gratinéed Potatoes in White Sauce

SERVES 6

6 cups La Ratte or fingerling potatoes

Salt as needed

2 tbsp unsalted butter

⅓ cup all-purpose flour

2 cups milk

1 clove

1 bay leaf

¼ medium onion

Salt and ground white or cayenne pepper as needed

Grated nutmeg as needed

¼ cup heavy cream

12 oz dry-cured bacon, sliced (16 slices)

1¼ cups grated Reblochon cheese

1 tbsp snipped chives

1. Preheat the oven to 450°F.

2. Wash the potatoes, place in a sauce pot, and cover them with cold water and a teaspoon of salt. Bring the potatoes to a boil and simmer for 20 minutes, or until they're cooked through. Drain and keep them warm.

3. To make the white sauce, melt the butter in a saucepan on medium heat, add the flour to form a roux, and cook it for 30 seconds while stirring constantly. Take the pan off the heat, and allow the roux to cool slightly. Add the milk and whisk until the roux is thoroughly dispersed into the milk. Return the pan to the stove and cook the mixture over medium heat. Stir the sauce continuously until it thickens, 5 to 10 minutes.

4. Insert the clove and bay leaf into the onion (this is called *onion piqué*), and add to the sauce. Cover the saucepan tightly with a lid or foil, and place it into a larger pan of simmering water for 30 minutes; the water should come to or above the level of the sauce in the smaller saucepan.

When the sauce is cooked, remove and discard the *onion piqué*. Season the sauce with salt, pepper, and nutmeg, and add the heavy cream. Keep the sauce warm in the water bath until needed.

5. Grill the bacon slices until they're crisp; cut them at right angles into ¼-inch strips. Cut the cooked potatoes into ¼-inch-thick slices.

6. In a bowl, mix the potatoes, four-fifths of the bacon, and enough sauce to lightly bind the two. Add half of the cheese and mix together thoroughly. Pour this mixture into a buttered 2-quart gratin dish. Top the mixture with the remaining sauce, cheese, and bacon and bake until it's golden brown, 15 to 20 minutes. Sprinkle the *tartiflette* with chives and serve.

◇◇◇◇◇◇◇◇◇◇◇◇◇◇◇◇◇◇◇◇◇◇◇◇◇

BEVERAGE: ALSACE PINOT GRIS RESERVE

Serve the *tartiflette* with a salad and a bottle of wine with some good acidity and enough body to stand up to this luxurious dish.

Galette de Pommes de Terre

Potato Cake

SERVES 6

3½ lb russet potatoes

2⅔ cups very thinly sliced shallots

1 tbsp chopped chives

Salt and pepper as needed

½ cup unsalted butter, melted

¼ cup clarified butter*

*For recipes and information about substitutions, see Fonds de Cuisine, page 175.

1. Peel the potatoes and cut them into long matchsticks or julienne, about 2 inches long. (Use either a mandolin or a grater for this job.) If grating, you'll need to squeeze out excess water at this stage. Combine the potatoes, shallots, and chives in a bowl. Season with salt and pepper. Pour the melted whole butter over them and mix well.

2. Heat a large sauté pan with the clarified butter. When hot, add the potato mixture and level it out evenly in the pan with the back of your spatula. Cook slowly over a moderate heat until the edges start become a golden color, about 15 minutes.

3. If you are adventurous you can flip the galette. If not, simply turn it over using a large spatula. One tricky turning method is to cover the sauté pan with a large dinner plate and flip the whole shebang over. Then slide the galette back into the pan, uncooked side down. Continue to cook until golden on the other side, about 15 minutes.

4. Turn the finished galette out onto a board and cut it into 6 servings. Serve immediately so you can enjoy while it's fresh, crisp, and hot!

Pommes de Terre Boulangère

Baked Potatoes and Onions

DISHES NAMED "BOULANGÈRE" have a unique relationship with bread bakers. At one time, bakers' ovens were also pressed into service as large, communal ovens. Families in a town would send casseroles like this one to go into the ovens after the bread baking was done, where they slowly baked for several hours in the residual heat.

SERVES 6

6 russet potatoes

2 large yellow onions, thinly sliced

Salt and pepper as needed

1 cup beef stock*

¼ cup unsalted butter, melted

1 tbsp chopped parsley

*For recipes and information about substitutions, see Fonds de Cuisine, page 175.

1. Preheat the oven to 350°F.

2. Peel the potatoes and slice them ⅛ inch thick. Reserve half of the slices for the top of the dish. Mix the rest of the slices in a bowl with the onions, then season with salt and pepper.

3. Place the mix into a buttered 9-inch by 13-inch baking dish. Neatly shingle the reserved slices of potato on top.

4. Boil the stock and pour enough over the potatoes to come halfway up. Brush the shingled top with the melted butter.

5. Bake in the oven for about 1 hour. Brush occasionally with butter during baking and moisten the top layer by pushing it down and allowing the stock to baste the potatoes.

6. The potatoes are cooked when they're golden brown on top and the bottom layers are soft. Remove the potatoes from the oven and sprinkle them with chopped parsley. Let them sit for a few minutes to allow the potatoes to absorb the stock. Serve while nice and hot.

CHAPTER FIVE

Entrées

Main Dishes

Sandwich de Saumon Fumé

Smoked Salmon Sandwich

THE FRENCH LIKE smoked salmon. Historically, 30 to 40 percent of salmon sold in the European Union go to smokers, and a good portion of the final product ends up in France. The classic accompaniments are on this open-faced sandwich. Don't skimp on the mayonnaise . . . its creaminess makes this simple preparation quite luxurious.

SERVES 4 AS A MAIN COURSE

¼ cup mayonnaise

2 tsp grated fresh horseradish, or to taste

½ tsp lemon juice

1 large hard-boiled egg

4 deli-sized slices pumpernickel bread

½ lb smoked salmon, sliced

1 large shallot, sliced

2 tbsp capers, rinsed of their brine

4 lemon wedges

1. Mix together the mayonnaise, horseradish, and lemon juice in a medium nonreactive bowl and set it aside for at least ½ hour so the flavors can mingle. If you can't get fresh horseradish, use 1 teaspoon of prepared horseradish.

2. Cut the egg with an egg slicer. Coat each slice of bread with one-quarter of the mayonnaise mixture.

3. Divide the smoked salmon among the 4 slices of bread. Place 2 or 3 slices of the egg on each sandwich slice of bread and garnish with the shallots and capers, and serve with a lemon wedge on the side.

◇◇◇◇◇◇◇◇◇◇◇

BEVERAGE: VOUVRAY

Smoked salmon is rich, so a balance needs to be struck with its accompaniments, including the wine. Vouvray, from a French village in the Loire, is made with the Chenin Blanc grape. This grape produces wines that can be dry or off dry, but despite how dry they are, almost all Vouvray wines have a bright acidity that is a perfect counterpart to the rich fish.

AT RIGHT: *Sandwich de Saumon Fumé (foreground) shown with Croque-Monsieur (background)*

Croque-Monsieur

"Crunch Mister" Sandwich

FOR DECADES, PARISIANS have depended on this delicious and affordable sandwich to sustain them from noon until dinnertime. Its name translates roughly to "crunch mister." Let's stick with the more romantic French name. The *croque-madame* is the same sandwich with a fried egg on top, although some say the *croque-madame* is a *croque-monsieur* with chicken replacing the ham.

While many versions of this sandwich exist, this one is just a bit more involved, and satisfying, than a simple grilled ham and cheese.

Dijon mustard as needed

8 slices country white bread

8 slices Jambon de Paris or good-quality
  boiled ham (½ lb)

8 slices Gruyère

3 tbsp unsalted butter, softened

2 cups Sauce Béchamel*

½ cup grated Gruyère

*For recipes and information about substitutions,
see Fonds de Cuisine, page 175.

1. Spread a thin layer of mustard on 4 of the bread slices. Divide the ham among those slices; cover the ham with the sliced Gruyère and the remaining bread slices.

2. Preheat a griddle or large sauté pan on medium heat and preheat the broiler. Butter the outsides of the sandwiches and place them in the hot pan. Turn them over after the first side is browned, 2 to 4 minutes, and cook the other side.

3. Smear ¼ cup of the béchamel sauce on top of each sandwich, and then scatter the grated Gruyère over the top. Place the sandwiches under the broiler until they are nicely browned on top, about 3 to 5 minutes. Allow them to rest for about 2 minutes before devouring.

◇◇◇◇◇◇◇◇◇◇◇◇◇◇◇◇◇◇◇◇◇◇◇◇◇◇◇◇

BEVERAGE: BEER OR AFFORDABLE ROSÉ

Since this is the staff of life for young travelers and students, serve it with what they drink the most. The beer should be crisp with decent body. If you opt for the rosé, it should be a little sweet. (I mean a little.)

Sandwich de Poulet Grillée

Grilled Chicken Sandwich

CHICKEN AND TARRAGON seem to have a predilection for each other, and this recipe puts them together in a simple way.

SERVES 4

4 boneless, skinless chicken breasts

FOR THE MARINADE:

⅓ cup olive oil

2 shallots, minced

1 tsp dried tarragon

Salt and pepper as needed

8 slices sourdough or country white bread

Mayonnaise as needed

1 medium tomato, sliced

1 bunch watercress, washed and dried

1. Lightly pound each chicken breast to even out its thickness.

2. Combine all of the marinade ingredients in a bowl and pour them into a 1-gallon-capacity plastic food-storage bag. Put the chicken breasts in the bag and seal. With the bag closed, massage it to coat all of the chicken breasts with the marinade. Refrigerate the breasts while getting the other ingredients ready.

3. Preheat the grill.

4. Remove the chicken from the marinade and let the excess oil drip off. Season the breasts with salt and pepper, and grill them, turning every few minutes, until they reach 160°F internal temperature, 12 to 14 minutes. Allow them to rest for 5 minutes while making the final preparations.

5. Slice the bread, if necessary, and toast it lightly. Spread mayonnaise over each slice of bread, and place tomato slices on 4 pieces of bread and watercress on the other four. Place a cooked chicken breast on the watercress side, assemble the sandwiches, and serve.

◇◇◇◇◇◇◇◇◇◇◇◇◇◇◇◇◇

BEVERAGE: GRAVES BLANC

Unlike the Sauvignon Blanc-based wines from the Loire Valley, in Bordeaux there is usually some Semillon and sometimes Muscadelle blended in, which can give this wine a little more body. With a sandwich like this, you don't want anything too serious, but it helps when the wine can hold its own, which the Graves will do.

L'HAMBURGER

Hamburger

❧

*I*S THE HAMBURGER FRENCH? Most likely, the French would argue vigorously that it is obviously not, but it *is* the most popular hot sandwich in the world and deserves a place in bistros. Now, how does a burger become *l'hamburger?* Well, you could plop a fried egg on top. Or perhaps you might cook the burger *bleu,* the rarest of rare, the way a Parisian would want it prepared. No, neither of these was what I wanted. I wanted French flavor, so I chose the best ingredients and used them thoughtfully to yield one of the best burgers I have ever eaten. Ever.

There really is only one absolute when it comes to producing a great burger: Don't manhandle the ground meat! Cooks who obsessively pat and compress the beef into tightly compacted pucks will get tough, dry burgers. Gently formed patties, with minimal handling, will be a little bit harder to deal with on the grill but the final product will be worth it. And finally, it doesn't make sense to use a crusty, firm bread roll with such a tender burger. A tender burger deserves tender bread, like egg rolls or even a brioche roll. Otherwise, the burger and toppings squirt out the back of the bread whenever you take a bite.

SERVES 6

2 lb ground beef, 85% lean

Salt and pepper as needed

¼ cup minced shallots

3 tbsp unsalted butter

½ cup Duxelles*

6 soft hamburger rolls

Blue cheese (such as Bleu d'Auvergne) as needed

4 tbsp mayonnaise

*For recipes and information about substitutions, see Fonds de Cuisine, page 175.

1. Gently form the ground meat into 6 patties. Season them liberally with salt and pepper. Preheat a cast-iron skillet or sauté pan large enough for the 6 burgers.

2. Place the minced shallots on a dinner plate. Lightly press each side of the hamburger patties into the shallots, so that each side gets an even distribution of shallots without covering the meat completely.

3. Melt the butter in the pan on medium heat; when the foam subsides put the patties in.

4. Warm up the duxelles. Split and toast the rolls. Spread the duxelles evenly among the 6 bottoms of the rolls.

5. While preparing the rolls, check the patties to see if they're browned. When well browned, after 5 to 7 minutes, turn them over. Don't worry if some of the shallots get a little burned. (This adds flavor.)

6. When the burgers are 5 minutes from your desired doneness, place the cheese on top and cover the pan to help the cheese melt.

7. Spread the mayonnaise on the tops of the rolls. When the burgers are done, place them on the roll bottoms (the duxelles will absorb the meat juices) and put the roll tops on. Cut the burgers in half and serve. Accompany them with *Pommes Frîtes* (page 71) or *Céleri Rémoulade* (page 67) and a watercress or arugula salad.

BEVERAGE: CORBIÈRES

This burger is big. Rich. A contender. Corbières is a wine from the Languedoc-Roussilion region that has a swagger in its step. Whether from the traditional Carignan grape, or some of the so-called "improving" varieties, like Syrah and Grenache, it is usually a spicy, dense wine that can easily deal with the fat and depth of flavor in this dish.

Sandwich d'Onglet

Open-Faced Hanger Steak Sandwich

WHILE MANY FRENCH are familiar with *l'onglet* as a type of steak, Americans are just now getting to know it as the hanger steak. It's not actually a cut of meat because the entire piece comes from near the steer's diaphragm, "hanging" between the rib and loin. With a somewhat large muscle grain and not much interior fat, it is very flavorful, but don't overcook this steak—rare or medium-rare is best. Known colloquially as a "butcher's cut," hanger steak used to be intended either for hamburger meat or for the butcher's dinner. I think it's worth following the lead of someone who knows a thing or two about the most flavorful cuts of meat. One to 1½ pounds of hanger steak will serve four lunch guests perfectly.

SERVES 4

MARINADE

1 large sprig rosemary

½ cup extra-virgin olive oil

3 garlic cloves

1½ lb hanger steak

1 large sweet onion

1 tbsp unsalted butter

1 tsp extra-virgin olive oil

Salt and pepper as needed

½ tsp sherry vinegar

4 thick slices country white or wheat bread

1 garlic clove, peeled

Extra-virgin olive oil to drizzle

1. Remove the leaves from the rosemary sprig and chop them finely, to about the size of match heads. Put the rosemary in a large plastic food-storage bag with the olive oil, and use a garlic press to squish the garlic cloves into the marinade. Mush the bag around to combine the ingredients and then put the steak into the bag. Seal the bag and massage the steak to coat it with the marinade. Refrigerate for at least an hour, although this can be done the night before.

2. Thinly slice the onion to yield about 2 cups. Heat a medium sauté pan on medium-low heat; add the butter, oil, and onions. Cook until the onions are soft and caramelized, about 15 minutes, adding drops of water if necessary to keep them somewhat fluid. Season with salt, pepper, and sherry vinegar. Set the onions aside and keep warm.

3. Preheat a grill or cast-iron skillet on high heat. Remove the steak from the marinade and allow it to drain a little, but leave enough marinade to flavor the steak and keep it from sticking to the pan. Cook the steak to just under the desired doneness and then allow it to rest, covered, for 5 minutes while doing final preparations.

4. Grill or toast the bread slices (you want a

few dark spots to really enjoy the smoky flavor). Rub each slice lightly with the garlic clove and drizzle it with a little olive oil. Spread the cooked onions over the bread slices and arrange them on a platter or individual plates.

5. Take the steak and cut it across the grain into thin slices. Divide the slices evenly onto the sandwiches and drizzle the accumulated juices from the resting platter. Accompany the sandwiches with a green salad or *Céleri Rémoulade* (page 67), or for a more substantial meal, with some sautéed bitter greens.

Saucisse à l'Ail aux Lentilles Vertes

Garlic Sausage on Green Lentils

SERVES 4 TO 6 AS AN APPETIZER

1 tbsp olive oil

1 large shallot, minced

1 cup dried green (du Puy) lentils, rinsed and drained

1 cup Chicken Stock*

2½ cups water

½ tsp salt

¼ tsp pepper

½ tsp sherry vinegar

½ lb saucisse à l'ail (French garlic sausage)

¼ cup chopped flat-leaf parsley

*For recipes and information about substitutions, see Fonds de Cuisine, page 175.

1. Heat the olive oil in a 3-quart saucepan on medium-high heat until shimmering but not smoking. Add the minced shallot and stir until it's fragrant, 3 to 4 minutes.

2. Add the lentils and stir for 1 to 2 minutes.

Add the stock and water and bring to a boil, then lower the heat and let simmer. Add the salt and cook, uncovered, stirring occasionally, for 25 to 35 minutes, or until lentils are tender.

3. Drain the lentils and reserve the cooking liquid. Return the liquid to the saucepan and reduce by half, or until slightly thickened, about 5 minutes. Return the lentils to the liquid, adjust the seasoning with salt and pepper, add the vinegar, and turn off the heat. Cover and set aside.

4. Heat the sausage by poaching (perhaps in reserved lentil liquid), steaming, or microwaving (use the highest power setting and keep the sausage covered with a paper towel on a plate). Slice the garlic sausage into ⅜-inch slices.

5. Divide the lentils onto warmed appetizer plates. Arrange the sausage slices over the top. Garnish with the parsley and serve.

◇◇◇◇◇◇◇◇◇◇◇◇◇◇◇◇◇◇◇◇◇◇◇◇◇

BEVERAGE: CRU BEAUJOLAIS (SUCH AS BROUILLY, FLEURIE, OR CHENAS)

This appetizer needs a red wine that is somewhat fresh. The *cru* Beaujolais wines are a little bit more serious than the *nouveau* styles, but should still be served slightly chilled.

Tronçon de Turbot aux Champignons Sauvages

Seared Turbot Steaks with Wild Mushrooms

A TRONÇON *IS* a fish steak cut at a 90-degree angle from half of a flat fish (usually a turbot or halibut). It traditionally includes the bone and skin. A cut across a round fish, such as salmon, is called a *darne*. They're both referred to as steaks in English, and are always cooked and served on the bone. There is no doubt that a fish cooked on the bone will give you a bigger flavor than a boneless cut, although you'll rarely find a restaurant in the United States that serves fish on the bone. We think that the extra work in eating fish cooked and served on the bone is more than repaid by the extra flavor and succulence.

SERVES 4

1 lb new potatoes, steamed until tender

4 turbot steaks (tronçon), 6 to 8 oz each

2 tbsp clarified butter*

Salt and pepper as needed

½ cup (8 tbsp) unsalted butter, divided use

⅓ cup finely minced shallots

½ garlic clove, crushed

3-½ cups assorted wild mushrooms, sliced

½ cup Sauvignon white wine

4 cups Fish Stock*

1 cup heavy cream

Lemon juice as needed

Chopped chervil, chives, parsley, and tarragon as needed (fines herbes)

*For recipes and information about substitutions, see Fonds de Cuisine, page 175.

1. Preheat the oven to 350°F. Cook the new potatoes in salted water for approximately 20 minutes, or until potatoes are cooked through. Drain and set them aside and keep warm.

2. Cook the fish and make the sauce while the potatoes are cooking. Heat the clarified butter in a large sauté pan over high heat. Season the turbot with salt and pepper and sear it for about 4 minutes on each side, or until they take on a good golden color. Place the seared *tronçons* on a cooking sheet and bake for approximately 10 minutes. The *tronçons* should reach an internal temperature of 135°F when done.

3. Heat 2 tablespoons of the butter in a medium skillet and add the shallots and garlic. Sweat over low heat for 2 minutes, or until shallots are translucent. Add the mushrooms and cook over moderate heat for another 2 minutes, until mushrooms start to soften and throw off some juice. Add the white wine (I used Domaine La Prevotes from Touraine) and reduce it by half, for about 4 minutes. Add the fish stock and reduce it over high heat by two-thirds, about

15 minutes. Add the cream and reduce until the sauce lightly coats the back of a spoon. Remove the pan from the burner.

4. Season the sauce with salt and pepper and add, while stirring, 2 tablespoons of butter. (We call this technique *monté au beurre*; see page 177.) Add a few drops of lemon juice, stir to combine, and keep the sauce warm.

5. Reheat the potatoes if necessary and slice them about ¼ inch thick. Shingle them around the outsides of the plates. With a slotted spoon, scoop out the mushrooms from the sauce and divide them evenly among the 4 plates (put them in the middle of the plate). Place the *tronçons* on top of the mushrooms and pour the remaining sauce over the fish.

6. Melt the remaining 4 tablespoons of butter in a small pan and add the fines herbes. Stir just enough to combine. Spoon this hot herb butter over the potatoes and serve.

◇◇◇◇◇◇◇◇◇◇◇◇◇◇◇◇◇◇◇◇◇◇◇◇◇◇

BEVERAGE: GEVREY-CHAMBERTIN

This meaty fish is nicely browned, with a wonderful and earthy mushroom sauce. This is the perfect opportunity to pair a red wine with fish. The fish and wild mushrooms are on the luxury end of the price scale, so don't skimp on the wine.

Turbot and halibut are flat fish, which means that the skin on one side of the fish is dark, while the other is light. That is the side that is constantly facing down toward the bottom of the ocean. If you have a sharp boning or fileting knife, preparing your own cuts of fish is very simple. Just buy a nice large piece of halibut or turbot, ideally a center cut, and then simply make cross cuts. If the fish is large, you may want to cut the entire piece in half lengthwise first.

SAUCE TARTARE

Tartar Sauce

———— ∞∞∞ ————

TARTAR SAUCE, when properly made, is a pungent, tart sauce. Capers and cornichons—tiny French-style pickles—and a combination of fresh herbs add texture and flavor. It's nothing like the bottled version.

MAKES 2½ CUPS SAUCE

¼ cup capers, rinsed and dried

¼ cup cornichons, rinsed and dried

½ bunch each of chervil, tarragon, chives, and parsley, stems removed

2 cups mayonnaise

2 tsp Dijon mustard

Worcestershire sauce as needed

Tabasco sauce as needed

1 tsp lemon juice

Salt and pepper as needed

Finely chop the capers, cornichons, and herbs. Mix these ingredients together in a medium bowl with the mayonnaise and mustard. Season to taste with Worcestershire, Tabasco, lemon juice, salt, and pepper. Hold the Tartar sauce in the refrigerator until you are ready to serve.

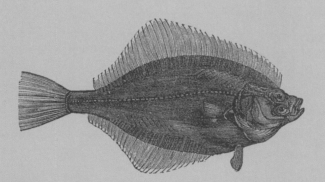

Goujonettes de Flet

Deep-Fried Flounder Strips

A GOUJON (FRENCH for "gudgeon") is a small, freshwater fish with a large head that tapers to a thin tail and is about 3 inches long. In the nineteenth century these fish were fried or baked with a puff pastry wrap, the head and tail pinched off before being eaten whole. The modern interpretation has come to describe a cut of fish. Here we're using flounder, but you could use any flat fish.

SERVES 6

1½ lb flounder fillet

Canola or peanut oil for frying

Salt and pepper as needed

1 cup all-purpose flour

4 large eggs, beaten with a pinch of salt

2¼ cups bread crumbs

Lemon wedges and parsley sprigs for garnish

Sauce Tartare (page 95)

1. Skin the fillets and cut them into several elongated triangles. Each piece should be about ½ inch wide at the wider end, tapering to a point, about 2 to 3 inches long.

2. Pour enough oil into a deep pot to fill it by 2 or 3 inches and heat to 360°F over moderate heat.

3. Meanwhile, season the fish with salt and pepper and dip it into the flour. Shake off the excess flour and dip the fish in the eggs. Drain off the excess egg and drop the fish into the bread-crumbs. Shake the pan to evenly coat the fish, and then gently shake the fish to remove the excess crumbs.

4. Use a frying basket if you have one: Place a few pieces of fish into the basket and lower the basket into the oil. Let the fish pieces fry until they're golden brown, about 3 minutes. Remove from the oil using the basket and blot them briefly on paper towels. (If you don't have a frying basket, use a slotted spoon or a spider to lower the fish into the oil. Don't use tongs, though, as they can pull off the breading.)

5. Place the *goujonettes* onto a doily-lined platter with lemon wedges and parsley sprigs, and tartare sauce on the side. Serve while they're hot!

◇◇◇◇◇◇◇◇◇◇◇◇◇◇◇◇◇◇◇◇◇◇◇

BEVERAGE: CRÉMANT DE LOIRE

Wines from the Loire go well with both freshwater and saltwater fish. Sparkling wines go famously with fried food. A perfect lesson in the old adage that the foods of the place are best accompanied by the wines of the same place.

Gibelotte de Lapin

Rabbit Stew

THIS DISH, AS with many others in this book, is accompanied by a reduction sauce. This method of cooking a sauce is done primarily to strengthen flavor and you must resist seasoning until the sauce has been reduced, otherwise your sauce may be too salty.

SERVES 6

2 rabbits (about 3½ to 4 lbs each)

MARINADE

2 sprigs each of rosemary, thyme, parsley, and tarragon

1 bay leaf

1 leek, cleaned and split lengthways

6 garlic cloves, peeled

2 tbsp white wine

4 tbsp olive oil

1 tsp finely chopped juniper berries

4 tbsp clarified butter*

1 cup finely chopped onions

1 cup finely chopped shallots

6 garlic cloves, finely chopped

2 cups dry white wine

1 cup crushed tomatoes

1 tsp tomato paste

4 cups Veal or Chicken Stock*

1 tbsp beurre manié, (see note on page 100)

Salt and pepper as needed

GARNISH

2 tbsp clarified butter*

1½ cups chanterelle mushrooms

3 tbsp chopped shallots

2 tsp chopped garlic

Salt and pepper as needed

1 tsp chopped parsley

*For recipes and information about substitutions, see Fonds de Cuisine, page 175.

1. Cut each rabbit into 6 pieces: 4 legs and the loin cut crossways in half. Fill each loin cavity with the herbs, leek, and garlic, which have been tied in bunches (bouquet garni), and then tie each loin to hold the bouquet in place (see photo opposite). Place the loin cavities and the legs into a glass or stainless steel dish. Pour the wine and olive oil over the rabbit and sprinkle with the juniper berries. Cover and marinate the rabbit in the refrigerator for 2 days.

2. Heat 2 tablespoons of clarified butter in a large, thick-bottomed pan over a medium flame. Sear the rabbit pieces, lightly browning all sides,

for 4 to 7 minutes per side. Remove the pieces to a plate and keep them warm. Add the remaining clarified butter and sauté the onions, shallots, and garlic until they're lightly browned, about 2 minutes. Add the wine, stirring to scrape up the fond, and reduce the liquid by half, about 7 minutes. Add the crushed tomatoes and tomato paste, and bring it to a boil.

3. Add the stock and seared rabbit pieces along with any juices that they have released; reduce the heat, bring the liquid to a gentle simmer, and cook slowly for 15 to 20 minutes. Remove the loins and keep them warm. Take out the bouquet garni from the loins, and return the bouquet to the sauce. Continue to cook the legs for about 10 more minutes or until they reach an internal temperature of 140°F, then remove and keep them warm with the loins.

4. Raise the heat and reduce the sauce until the desired taste is achieved, about 8 to 10 minutes. Whisk pea-size pieces of the *beurre manié* into the sauce, boiling the sauce between additions, until you have a light coating sauce. Season to taste with salt and pepper.

5. Cut the loins in half crosswise and return them, along with the rabbit legs, to the sauce and keep it all warm.

6. For the garnish, heat 2 tablespoons of clarified butter on high heat in a medium sauté pan. Sauté the mushrooms for 2 minutes, then add the shallots and garlic. Continue to sauté for 2 minutes, until the mushrooms are tender and the shallots are translucent. Be careful not to burn the shallots and garlic. Season as needed with salt and pepper.

7. Place the rabbit pieces into a serving dish and pour the sauce over them. Garnish the dish with the sautéed mushrooms, sprinkle with parsley, and serve.

◇◇◇◇◇◇◇◇◇◇◇◇◇◇◇◇◇◇

BEVERAGE: RHÔNE REDS

Rustic rabbit stew is one of my favorite dinners. While the meat itself is rather neutral, the herbs and wild mushrooms are just begging for a spicy, but not overpowering red wine. For this, we should head to one of the less-known parts of the Rhône, like St. Joseph or Vacqueyras. The reds from there will still be spicy and fun, but won't weigh down the dish.

◇◇◇◇

NOTE:

Beurre manié is simply equal parts butter and flour mixed to a soft paste and used as a last-minute thickening agent.

Aiguillettes de Canard aux Cerises

Sliced Duck Breast with Cherries

THIS IS A quick and delicious way to enjoy *magret*. These enlarged breasts, or *suprêmes*, are from ducks that are raised for foie gras, and are usually large enough to serve two people.

SERVES 4

2 magret duck breasts (suprêmes)

1 tbsp clarified butter*

4 tbsp Armagnac

1 tbsp red wine vinegar

1 tbsp red currant jelly

⅔ cup port

Zest and juice of 1 sweet navel orange

2 cups Demi-glace*

Salt and pepper as needed

1 lb fresh sour cherries, stoned

*For recipes and information about substitutions, see Fonds de Cuisine, page 175.

1. Preheat the oven to 350°F. If the two magrets are joined, separate them by cutting on either side of the center line to remove the tough cartilage. Score the fat of the breasts in a crisscross pattern to render the fat when searing.

2. In a large, thick-bottomed skillet, heat the butter over low heat and add the magrets, fat side down. Cook them slowly for 5 to 8 minutes until a good amount of the fat has rendered into the pan and you have a golden, crisp, checkered skin. Check the color during this rendering process and turn the heat down if they're getting too dark too quickly.

3. Turn the breasts over and cook for another minute or so. Pour off the rendered fat and transfer the breasts to a baking dish. Finish cooking the duck in the oven for 6 to 8 minutes. Remove from the oven and keep warm.

4. While the duck is cooking, make the sauce. In a pan, reduce the Armagnac over low heat until almost it's almost dry. Add the vinegar and jelly and reduce the sauce to a sticky syrup, 4 to 5 minutes. Add the port and reduce it by half. Add the orange juice and a pinch of zest and reduce that by half. Add the demi-glace and reduce it all until the sauce lightly coats the back of a spoon.

5. Season the sauce with salt and pepper and add the cherries. Cook it over a low heat just enough to soften the cherries and keep the sauce warm, about 2 minutes. Do not let it boil.

6. Carve the duck breasts lengthwise into ⅛-inch slices (see note). Arrange the duck slices on plates and coat with cherry sauce.

◇◇◇◇◇◇◇◇

CHEF'S NOTE:

Because the duck skin is crispy, it's often easier to carve the duck upside down. This allows you to cut through the pink meat, a thin layer of fat, and finally the crispy skin.

Canard à l'Orange

Duck in Orange Sauce

THIS IS A classic combination of rich duck perfectly complimented by a zesty orange sauce.

SERVES 6

2 ducklings (3 lbs each)

6 navel oranges

1 lemon

⅓ cup sugar

5 tbsp red wine vinegar

2½ pt Brown Veal Stock*

¼ cup clarified butter*

Salt and pepper as needed

4 tbsp Grand Marnier

*For recipes and information about substitutions, see Fonds de Cuisine, page 175.

1. Preheat the oven to 400°F. Cut the legs and wings away from the ducks. Cut down both sides of the backbone, removing the breast portion from the backbone and separating the collar bone from the meat by cutting through the joint. Put the legs and breasts to the side. Remove all skin and fat from the back bones. Brown the bones and wings in the oven for 30 to 40 minutes. Reserve.

2. Use a peeler to remove the zest from 2 of the oranges and the lemon. Carefully cut off any pith and julienne the zest. Blanch the zest in boiling water for 30 seconds, strain, and reserve. Juice 4 of the oranges and the lemon. Peel and segment the remaining 2 oranges; make sure all of the skin and pith are removed.

3. To make the sauce, cook the sugar in a large skillet over medium heat until it is a golden color, about 2 or 3 minutes. Add the red wine vinegar and reduce until nearly dry without stirring. Quickly add the citrus juices, veal stock, and browned duck bones and bring it to a boil. Simmer gently for 40 minutes to form a stock.

4. Lower the oven to 350°F. Sear the duck breasts and legs in clarified butter in a large sauté pan over high heat until they're golden, about 10 minutes. Transfer them to a roasting pan, season with salt and pepper, and roast in the oven for 40 minutes, until they're golden. Remove and keep them warm.

5. Pour off the fat and deglaze the pan juices with the Grand Marnier. Remove the bones from the stock and discard. Pour the deglazed juices from the roasting pan into the stock, increase the heat to high, and reduce the sauce to your desired taste. When the sauce lightly coats the back of a spoon and has good flavor, pass it through a fine strainer. Season with salt and pepper and add the zests and orange segments.

6. Cut each duck breast into two pieces by cutting cross-ways through thickest portion of the breast. Separate the legs into thighs and drumsticks by cutting through the joint. Pour the sauce over the duck making sure to include some of the segments and zest in each portion. Serve immediately.

Confit de Canard

Duck Confit

IDEALLY FOR THIS DISH, use legs from ducks that have been reared for foie gras, because they have a higher yield of meat and fat.

The fat is used to cover the duck during cooking and storage. Confit is a method used for preserving the duck and holding it fresh for later use. The duck is submerged in fat, keeping it away from air and bacteria. This fat can be used many times for cooking confit. It is strained after each use and kept in the refrigerator.

SERVES 6

6 duck legs

DRY CURE FOR DUCK LEGS

1 cup kosher salt

½ cup chopped garlic

1 bunch thyme, picked

10 bay leaves, crushed

1 tbsp black peppercorns, crushed

5 lb fatty duck skins (or 4 lb duck fat)

1. To cure the duck legs, remove the thigh bones but leave the thigh meat attached to the legs. Trim off the excess fat from around the legs and set it aside. You should save all the fat and skin to add during the rendering step listed below. Mix all of the cure ingredients together in a bowl. Sprinkle half of the mix onto the bottom of a nonreactive pan. Lay the duck legs on top of the cure and cover them with the remainder of the cure. Cure the legs overnight in the refrigerator. The next day, scrape the excess cure from the legs and wash them well under cold running water.

2. To render the fat from the duck skins, place them in a large, heavy pot with ¼ cup of water. Simmer over moderate heat until the skin is browned and crisp (cracklings), about 1 hour and 15 minutes. Strain the fat into a storage bowl, and either use it right away to make the confit or cool it and store in the fridge.

3. To make the confit, place the cured duck legs into a large, thick-bottomed saucepan and pour enough duck fat over the legs to submerge them. Cook the legs over a *very* low heat for approximately 1½ hours, or until the duck is fork tender. When the duck begins to brown slightly, it usually indicates it's ready. Remove from the heat and store the cooked duck in a crock or bowl, covered with the duck fat, in the refrigerator for up to 3 weeks. When you're ready to finish your duck legs, simply pull them from the fat and scrape the excess back into the dish for when you want to make confit again.

Confit avec Pruneaux et Pommes

Duck Confit with Prunes and Apples

THIS DISH IS a study in contrasts: rich, unctuous duck confit, enrobed crisp, crackly skin is paired with sweet dried and fresh fruits, and a sauce redolent with Armagnac—a collection of as many of the glories of Gascon cuisine as we could fit on a single plate.

SERVES 6

6 legs Duck Confit (page 103)

1 tbsp clarified butter,* plus more as needed

⅓ cup diced prunes

½ cup diced Pippin apples

¼ cup chopped walnuts

2 or 3 tablespoons duck fat (from confit)

12 fingerling potatoes, steamed until tender and halved lengthwise

1¾ cups chanterelle mushrooms

Salt and pepper as needed

Red grapes, halved, as needed

1 cup Armagnac Sauce (page 106)

Sea salt and cracked black peppercorns as needed

4 cups mesclun lettuce mix, rinsed and dried

*For recipes and information about substitutions, see Fonds de Cuisine, page 175.

1. Preheat the oven to 400°F. Remove the cured legs from the duck fat, scraping off any excess. Set them on a rack on a baking sheet to catch any fat and put in the oven for about 20 minutes, or until they begin to turn golden-brown.

2. As the duck is reheating, heat a tablespoon of butter and add the prunes, apples, and walnuts. Stir over medium heat until the ingredients are very warm, but they should not take on any color.

3. Heat 2 tablespoons of the rendered duck fat in a large sauté pan over medium heat. Add the fingerling potatoes and sauté, cut side down, until golden brown, about 10 minutes. Watch them as they cook—you may need to flip a few over as they sauté. Remove them

(recipe continues on next page)

with a slotted spoon and transfer to a warm dish. Sauté the mushrooms in the same pan, adding more duck fat if needed, until they're golden, 4 to 5 minutes; season them with salt and pepper.

4. To serve, arrange the potatoes at the back of the plate, and the mushrooms directly in front of them; use this as a platform for the duck leg to rest against. Garnish the dish with grapes and add the prune mixture, then drizzle sauce around the plate. Season with the sea salt and freshly cracked black pepper as needed, add a bit of mesclun behind the duck leg, and serve.

Armagnac Sauce

MAKES 1 CUP

2 tsp vegetable oil

*1 cup mirepoix (½ cup diced onion, ¼ cup diced
    carrot, ¼ cup diced celery)*

4 tsp tomato paste

¼ cup red wine

¼ cup brandy

5 cups Veal Stock*

1 sachet*

4 oz browned beef trim (optional)

½ tsp cracked black peppercorns

2 tbsp Armagnac

Salt as needed

*For recipes and information about substitutions, see Fonds de Cuisine, page 175.

1. Heat the oil in a medium saucepan on high heat to smoking point. Add the mirepoix and caramelize it, about 3 minutes, but do not allow it to burn. Add the tomato paste and cook until it releases a sweet aroma and turns a rusty color, 1 to 2 minutes.

2. Add the red wine and stir to deglaze the pan. Add the brandy and simmer the liquid over medium heat until it reduces by half, about 2 to 4 minutes. Add the stock, sachet, and beef trim (if using). Reduce the sauce to the desired consistency, 40 to 50 minutes (it should lightly coat the back of a spoon).

3. Strain the sauce, and then add the peppercorns and Armagnac. Season the sauce as needed with salt. Keep warm. (You can cool the sauce and store in the refrigerator for up to 1 week. Bring the sauce to a simmer over medium heat before serving if necessary.)

◇◇◇◇◇◇◇◇◇◇◇◇◇◇◇◇◇◇◇◇◇◇◇◇◇

**BEVERAGE: COTE ROTIE, BORDEAUX,
OR BURGUNDY**

You want a wine with a medium-heavy body to match the duck, pronounced flavor to stand up to the rich flavor, and a good acidity to combat the fat and refresh the palate. A Cote Rotie, or the finest Bordeaux or Burgundy, would make the perfect accompaniment to this dish.

Cassoulet

IF YOU EVER want to start a bistro fight in southwest France, walk into a local watering hole and start talking about how cassoulet should be made. While Americans feud over whether chili con carne should have beans (Texans say never) or tomato (which Texans also eschew), cassoulet cooks argue over even the basic ingredients, for the most part only agreeing on the presence of both meat and beans.

Most cooks will agree that cassoulet is from the Languedoc region of France, but which town? The Toulouse version, with its sausage and confit, is probably the most famous. However, Castelnaudary is often mentioned as the home of cassoulet, where a more elemental version holds sway, with only pork products joining the white beans. The third town that lays claim to the true cassoulet is Carcassonne, where mutton joins the party, along with the odd partridge during hunting season. Perhaps the best treatment of this subject is in Paula Wolfert's updated classic book, *The Cooking of Southwest France*.

SERVES 6 TO 8 AS A MAIN COURSE

2 lb dried white beans, soaked overnight, or 3 cans (19 oz each)

¼ cup rendered duck fat (see note on page 109)

½ lb pancetta, in one slice

1 lb fresh and whole pork belly, cut into 1-inch by 2-inch rectangles

1 lb boneless pork butt, cut into 2-inch cubes

3 canned plum tomatoes, or 2 tbsp concentrated tomato paste

3 carrots, peeled and cut into large dice

2 medium onions, cut into large dice

1 shallot, cut into small dice

7 garlic cloves

2 qt Chicken Stock* or water (or combination of both)

3 sprigs parsley

3 sprigs thyme

1 celery stalk, cut into 3 sections

2 bay leaves

¼ tsp black pepper

4 legs Duck Confit (page 103)

1 lb garlic sausage

½ cup bread crumbs

*For recipes and information about substitutions, see Fonds de Cuisine, page 175.

1. Preheat a 5½-quart enameled cast-iron casserole on low heat. Either add the duck fat to the pot or slowly render any excess fat from the outsides of the duck legs, if the duck confit was purchased. If store bought, remove the legs once they're browned. Brown the pancetta in the duck fat on medium heat, about 3 minutes. Remove with a slotted spoon and set it aside on a paper towel to drain. Do the same with the belly and butt pieces, 8 to 10 minutes each. Add the tomatoes or paste to the casserole and cook until it smells sweet. Add the carrots, onions,

shallot, and 5 cloves of peeled garlic. Stir occasionally and allow the vegetables to lightly brown, about 10 minutes, but do not burn the fond. When the vegetables are browned and softened, add the stock or water, meats, parsley, thyme, celery, bay leaves, and black pepper into the stew. Bring it to a boil, and then lower to a simmer. Cook for 1 hour.

2. In the meantime, drain the soaking beans (skip this step if using canned beans and add them to the stew in Step 3). Add the beans to the stew. Cook the stew at a slow simmer until the beans are cooked, about 2 hours. Remove the stew from the heat and allow it to cool for about an hour.

3. If forging ahead with the cassoulet, remove the fat from the surface of the stew and reserve 4 tablespoons of it. If finishing the dish the next day, cover the stew and refrigerate. The next day, remove the solidified pork fat from the surface of the stew and reserve 4 tablespoons of it. Allow the stew to warm up a bit (add canned beans to the stew at this point), and remove and discard the parsley, thyme, celery, and bay leaves. Pull out the pancetta, cut off the excess fat and cut it into 1½-inch chunks. Return it to the pot.

4. Preheat the oven to 350°F. Warm up the duck legs (either by microwave, briefly, or steam) to make it easier to take the meat off the bones in chunks, and then put the chunks in the casserole. Peel the last 2 garlic cloves, push them through a garlic press, and stir them into the stew. Cook the stew in the oven until it's heated through (165°F), from 1 to 2 hours, depending on the cooking vessel.

5. Brown the garlic sausage in a sauté pan and cut it into 2½-inch chunks. Pull the casserole from the oven and give it a stir. Place the sausage chunks on top and cover the surface with bread crumbs. Drizzle with the reserved pork fat.

6. Lower the oven to 275°F and return the cassoulet to bake, uncovered. When the crust is lightly browned on top, after 18 to 20 minutes, lightly break up the crust and push it just below the surface of the liquid. If desired, repeat several times until a thick crust forms, and the casserole is well browned on top.

7. Remove the casserole from the oven and allow it to rest for about 30 minutes while it thickens up a bit. When serving, make sure each guest gets a little bit of the crust, and at least one piece of each kind of meat. Oh, and some beans, too.

◇◇◇◇◇◇◇

BEVERAGE:

Look for a wine similar to a Pinot Noir to enjoy with this substantial dish with its hint of spiciness: the flavors of cloves, geranium, and black cherries.

◇◇◇◇

NOTE:

This recipe is a fairly faithful rendition of the Toulouse version of cassoulet. There are two options we give you here that can drastically cut down the time it takes to prepare: the use of canned beans and prepared duck leg confit. Purists may have just thrown this book on the floor, but for those of you still reading, three days of intermittent effort is too much to ask of most cooks in America today. Of the two shortcuts, buying prepared confit is, by far, the biggest time-saver.

Prepared duck confit is readily available from a number of sources, and will not diminish the quality of the final product, although it might cut down on bragging rights.

While preparation can be compressed into one busy day, it's actually easier to make the pork and bean stew one day and finish it the next (in particular because you can remove extra fat from the stew more easily and completely).

Coq au Vin

Rooster Cooked in Red Wine

WHEREVER THERE'S A CHICKEN FARM, there's a recipe for old chickens in a pot. Of course, this recipe, at least in name, demands the use of an old rooster who has outlived his usefulness on the farm.

Sadly, making true *coq au vin* with a rooster in this country poses a distinct challenge to the cook, in these days of the modern, tender supermarket chicken. But you still have some options available to make something close to the original.

For more flavor, you can use a stewing hen or fowl, which many specialty markets and even larger grocery stores carry for making soup and stock. The meat will be tougher, of course, but the long cooking time for coq au vin results in tender, melt-in-your mouth textures.

What if there are no roosters, or even stewing hens, available to you? Although you won't really be making a coq au vin, you can prepare a version of this dish with a good-quality free-range chicken and shorten the cooking time. While red wine is the right choice for older birds (with sturdier bones) because they have more flavor, younger, more delicate chickens are best prepared with white wine and the bacon omitted to prepare *poulet au vin blanc*. Serve this dish with buttered noodles, or boiled or mashed potatoes.

SERVES 6 TO 8 AS A MAIN COURSE

1 rooster, stewing hen, or stewing fowl (about 6 lb)

1 carrot, chopped

1 celery stalk, chopped

1 medium onion, chopped roughly

5 oz slab bacon or pancetta, unsliced

1 tsp unsalted butter

Salt and pepper as needed

24 pearl onions, peeled

12 small white mushrooms, whole (about the size of the pearl onions)

1 medium onion, cut into large dice

2 carrots, cut into large dice

1 celery stalk, cut into large dice

3 garlic cloves

2 tbsp all-purpose flour, toasted*

2 tbsp brandy

1 bottle full-bodied red wine (750 ml)

3 sprigs thyme

2 bay leaves

1 tbsp butter

*For recipes and information about substitutions, see Fonds de Cuisine, page 175.

1. Cut the rooster into 8 serving pieces. Reserve the breast and leg pieces and use the back, wings, and giblets to prepare a stock.

2. To make the stock, add the back, wings, and giblets (except the liver) to a small stockpot with the chopped carrot, celery stalk, and onion. Cover the contents with cool water and bring it to a very low simmer. Simmer for about 2 hours. Skim the surface occasionally to remove impurities. This stock will be used later in the dish, so keep it warm on the stove until you need it, in step 7.

3. Cut the bacon or pancetta into lardons (see page 178). Unsmoked bacon is preferable to give the final dish a cleaner flavor, but smoked bacon is better than no bacon. Put the lardons into an enameled, 5½-quart cast-iron casserole with 1 teaspoon of butter. Cook gently on medium-low heat until the fat is rendered and the pancetta or bacon is medium brown but not yet crispy, about 6 minutes. Remove the lardons with a slotted spoon and set them aside to drain on a paper towel.

4. Season the rooster pieces on both sides with salt and pepper, and brown them in the pork fat on medium heat, about 4 minutes on each side. Don't crowd the pan, but more importantly, don't scorch the fond that is forming; it will be the basis of the sauce. Remove the browned rooster pieces and set them aside on a warm plate. Remove all but 2 tablespoons of the fat in the pan, and reserve what you removed.

5. In the same casserole, sear the pearl onions and mushrooms separately until lightly browned. Remove with a slotted spoon and transfer to bowls; reserve. Add the diced onion, carrot, and celery to the casserole and cook on medium until the onion is deep brown, about 10 to 12 minutes. Crush the garlic cloves with the side of a chef's knife, pull away the peels, and add them to the casserole. Cook the mix until the garlic is fragrant, about 3 minutes.

6. Sift the flour into the vegetables. Cook until evenly combined (it will look a little pasty), 1 to 3 minutes. Remove from the heat and let it cool for about 5 minutes. Deglaze with the brandy and wine, stirring to loosen any drippings that have begun to stick to the pan, and evenly blend in the flour. Add the thyme and bay leaves, and return the rooster (with its juices) and lardons to the pan.

7. Add the stock to the casserole so it just covers the rooster pieces. Bring the stock to a boil, then lower the heat to establish a simmer. Cook, partially covered, for 1 hour, then add the pearl onions and cook another 45 minutes. When the rooster is tender, but not falling off the bone, remove the pieces and keep warm. Reduce the sauce to a slightly syrupy consistency, about 10 minutes, and swirl in 1 tablespoon of butter. Add the mushrooms and return the rooster to the sauce to heat it through.

8. Serve the rooster pieces coated with the sauce and the vegetables.

◇◇◇◇◇◇◇

BEVERAGE:

Whatever red wine you put in the stew, pick a more expensive version of that wine, or grape, to put in the glasses. For example, if you used Côtes du Rhône for cooking, serve your rooster with a Gigondas or Saint-Joseph.

Paillards

Scallops of Chicken, Veal, or Swordfish

ONE OF THE CLASSIC quick lunch (or dinner) meals in casual French restaurants is a grilled paillard with a green salad and some matchstick potatoes. *Paillard* comes from the same root word that means "straw mattress." As you might guess, when it comes to cooking, the straw mattress is a description of the dish, made from tender cuts of meat, fish, or poultry that have been pounded. In fact, the majority of your cooking time is spent pounding out the paillards, which can be done earlier in the day or even the day before. If pounded in advance, store the paillards in their original plastic wrap and refrigerate. Now all you'll have to make is a salad and some matchstick fries. Frankly, you can buy the potatoes if you're truly in a rush, but homemade are a nice touch. The actual grilling time is less than five minutes.

Choosing a vinaigrette for the meat (and salad) is pretty easy—tarragon is great with all three, but especially chicken. The veal would be nice with a sun-dried tomato version, and the swordfish with fresh oregano. Obviously, any of these choices would be fine with all three protein options . . . go with whatever you like! You could also top any of the paillards with a teaspoon of maître d'hôtel compound butter.

SERVES 4 AS A MAIN COURSE (RECIPE CAN BE EASILY INCREASED)

Four 4-oz portions of either boneless and
*   skinless chicken breasts, veal medallions,*
*   or swordfish steaks*

Olive oil as needed

⅔ cup Balsamic Vinaigrette*, or chef's choice

4 cups salad greens

Pommes Frites (page 71)

Vegetable oil as needed

Salt and pepper as needed

*For recipes and information about substitutions, see Fonds de Cuisine, page 175.

1. Brush a protein portion generously with olive oil on both sides. Pull out a piece of plastic wrap about twice as long as it is wide, and lay it down on the work surface. Place the protein on the half closest to you. Fold the top half of the wrap towards you and smooth it out.

2. Pound out the meat with the smooth side of a meat pounder or scaloppine hammer. Avoid using the tenderizer side (with ridges or points)—it can tear the plastic wrap and make small holes in the flesh. Work from the center to the edges, occasionally smoothing it out to make sure the meat or fish is an even thickness all over. Thick spots might stay undercooked.

3. Repeat with the other portions. If you're going to store them, leave them in their plastic wrap and stack on a dinner plate, then cover with another piece of wrap before putting them in the refrigerator.

4. Heat a charcoal or gas grill (or a cast iron grill pan in the winter). You'll want a very hot fire, which you'll need for a very short time. Make sure the grill is very clean.

5. Prepare the vinaigrette, salad, and fries while the grill is heating. Place the salad and fries onto the dinner plates right before you grill the meat.

6. Wipe some vegetable oil on the grates of the grill using a rag or paper towel. Open the plastic wrap on the top paillard. Brush with additional olive oil and season with salt and pepper. Slide your hand underneath and then flip the paillard over and onto the hot grill. Be careful not to let plastic wrap touch the grill. Repeat with the remaining paillards. Let the meat cook, untouched, until it releases from the grill grates, about 3 minutes. Flip with a large offset spatula, and wait again for the meat to release, about 2 more minutes.

7. Move the paillards to dinner plates already set up with salad and fries and drizzle 1 tablespoon of vinaigrette onto them.

◇◇◇◇◇◇◇◇◇◇◇◇◇◇◇◇◇◇◇

OPTIONS FOR SERVING:

1. Place the cooked paillards directly on top of the salad and omit the potatoes. Serve with bread (or not, for you low-carb types).

2. Put the dressed salad on top of the paillard and serve potatoes on the side.

3. Dress the salad with a vinaigrette, put the paillard alongside with a vegetable or fruit salsa on top.

4. Use your imagination and do whatever you want.

◇◇◇◇◇◇◇

BEVERAGE:

Sauvignon Blanc or Rhône varietals are good choices (of course, the final selection depends upon what you are grilling). Look for wines with the flavors of herbs, red fruit, or black pepper.

Poêlé de Chapon

Butter-Roasted Capon

A TRADITIONAL POÊLÉ can be made with almost any white meat, poultry, or game bird. The dish gets its name from the cooking pan. The pan is tightly closed throughout cooking time so that the meat's natural juices can baste the food as it cooks.

To *poêlé* is to roast in a covered dish (casserole, pot, etc., or whatever one calls the vessel). The concept, as with other sealed cooking methods, is to retain all the flavor and rendered juices from the meat. These juices caramelize into the bed of mixed vegetables and ham which surrounds the meat, known as a *matignon*.

Capons, featured in this recipe, are castrated male chickens. They yield a flavorful but still tender meat, and are large enough to serve a small dinner party. Accompany with whatever you like, but there is a lot of merit in following established custom: The traditional potatoes that are served with this dish are called *cocottes,* which are small turned potatoes that are browned in butter and added to the pot in the last 20 minutes.

SERVES 6 AS A MAIN COURSE

1 whole capon (6 to 9 lb)

3 tarragon sprigs

8 tbsp (1 stick) salted butter, soft

2 large carrots, peeled

2 celery stalks

1 large onion, peeled

Salt and pepper as needed

3 oz diced ham

3 tbsp toasted flour*

¾ cup white wine

2 cups Demi-glace or 4 cups Chicken Stock*,
    reduced by half*

2 tbsp salted butter, cold

*For recipes and information about substitutions, see Fonds de Cuisine, page 175.

1. Wash the capon in cold water and pat dry with paper towels. Don't forget to remove the package containing the neck and giblets from the body cavity. Cut off the wing tips and add them to your "stock pile."

2. Pull the tarragon leaves off their sprigs and set aside. Preheat the oven to 375°F. Work your fingers under the skin that covers the breast meat. In a small bowl, combine 3 tablespoons of the softened butter with the tarragon leaves and mix by hand. Rub this mixture under the skin onto the breast meat.

3. Cut the carrots and celery into 1-inch pieces, and quarter the onion. Season the cavity of the

bird with salt and pepper. Season the outside of the bird well with salt and pepper. Rub 3 to 4 tablespoons of the softened butter all over the skin, and set the capon aside while you proceed with the preparation of the *matignon*.

4. Heat a Dutch oven or flameproof casserole over medium-high heat. Add 1 or 2 tablespoons of the butter and melt. Add the onions, carrots, celery, and ham to the Dutch oven and cook, stirring, until the onions are tender and translucent. Season with a little salt and pepper.

5. Put the bird on top of the matignon and cover the Dutch oven or casserole tightly. Place in the oven and cook, basting the bird regularly, about every 20 or 25 minutes. After the capon has roasted for about 90 minutes, check its internal temperature with an instant-read thermometer. When the thermometer registers 160°F in the joint between the thigh and the leg, remove the bird to a platter and cover it with foil. Allow the capon to rest while you make the gravy.

6. Put the Dutch oven or casserole over high heat. Spoon out most of the fat from the pan, leaving behind a tablespoon or so (save this richly flavored fat to sauté vegetables or potatoes). Whisk in the flour and cook until the flour loses its raw smell and turns lightly brown, about 5 minutes. Add the wine and scrape up the browned bits from the bottom of the pan.

7. Add the demi-glace or reduced chicken stock and the accumulated juices from the resting bird and reduce until it's the consistency of half-and-half, 10 to 15 minutes. The gravy should not be too thick, nor too watery.

8. When you are ready to serve the capon, whisk the 2 tablespoons of cold butter into the sauce and matignon to add sheen, consistency, and flavor. Adjust seasoning as needed with salt and pepper.

9. Carve the bird either in the kitchen or at the table. Serve the sauce and matignon.

◇◇◇◇◇◇◇◇◇◇◇◇◇◇◇◇◇◇◇◇◇◇◇◇◇◇◇◇◇◇◇◇◇◇

BEVERAGE: BOURGOGNE, EITHER WHITE OR RED

Few main dishes are as flexible with wine as a roast chicken (or capon), and this poêléed capon is a fitting partner for that special bottle in your cellar (or in my case, basement). If you'd like the white option, try to get a fuller-bodied wine with some oak. If you prefer a red Burgundy, almost any one will do, just pick one that will make you happy.

Oeufs en Meurette

Eggs Poached in Red Wine Sauce

IN THIS DISH, eggs are poached in a rich red wine sauce, garnished with garlic croutons, lardons, and mushrooms. Use the freshest eggs you can find, ideally from free-range local birds, paired with a good-quality red Burgundy wine to really appreciate this unique marriage of flavors.

This dish is a favorite in Burgundy. My colleagues and I were fortunate enough to enjoy this incredible dish as an appetizer at a small bistro in Beaune, a quintessential wine town. I wanted to include it as a main dish perfect for a Sunday supper *en famille*.

SERVES 4

FOR THE POACHING SAUCE:

¼ cup finely chopped bacon

4 shallots, finely chopped

¾ cup finely chopped carrots

1 bouquet garni*

3½ cups good-quality red Burgundy wine

4 cups Chicken* or Veal Stock*, reduced to 2 cups

½ cup slab bacon (4 oz), cut into lardons (see page 178)

1¼ cups quartered white mushrooms

1 tsp all-purpose flour

¼ cup unsalted butter

Salt and pepper as needed

8 large eggs

16 Garlic Croutons*

1 tbsp chopped parsley

*For recipes and information about substitutions, see Fonds de Cuisine, page 175.

1. To make the poaching sauce, render the bacon in a large saucepan over medium heat for about 3 minutes. When the bacon is crisp, add the shallots and carrots and cook until softened, about 8 minutes. Add the bouquet garni and the wine; bring the sauce to a boil and reduce by half, about 30 minutes. Add the reduced chicken or veal stock and boil for another 10 minutes.

2. Preheat the oven to 350°F. While you're waiting for the poaching sauce, prepare the garnish: Sauté the lardons of bacon in a medium saucepan over medium heat until just crisp, about 5 minutes. Remove the lardons from the pan with a slotted spoon, place them on a plate, and add the mushrooms to the pan. Sauté until cooked, about 5 minutes; remove the mushrooms from the pan and add to the plate with the lardons.

3. When the poaching sauce has thickened somewhat to a light nappé consistency (thick enough to coat a wooden spoon), pour it through a fine-mesh strainer into another small sauté pan.

4. Make the *beurre manié* by working together the flour and 1 teaspoon of the butter to make a soft, smooth paste. Season the poaching sauce as needed with salt and pepper. To thicken it

slightly, add the *beurre manié* a little bit at a time to the simmering sauce off the heat, whisking to blend it into the sauce evenly. Whisk the remaining butter into the poaching sauce to enrich it.

5. When the sauce reaches a poaching temperature (165°F), keep the heat under the pan very low. Crack the eggs straight into the sauce and poach them until the white is set but the yolks are runny, 6 to 8 minutes.

6. Carefully transfer 2 eggs per person into *sur-le-plat* dishes or small side plates. Add the lardons and mushrooms to the poaching sauce and spoon this over the eggs to coat. Garnish the dish with the garlic croutons, 3 or 4 around the eggs, and sprinkle with chopped parsley. Serve with some of the Burgundy wine that was used for the sauce.

◇◇◇◇◇◇◇◇◇◇◇◇◇◇◇◇◇◇◇◇◇◇◇◇◇◇◇

BEVERAGE: BOURGOGNE ROUGE

Because this egg recipe is so rich, opt for something from the Côte de Nuits, like a Côte de Nuits-Villages. Reds from there tend to have more power than those from other parts of Burgundy.

Choucroute in Paris

CHOUCROUTE, A DISTINCTLY unsophisticated dish, came to the attention of the French after the Peace of Westphalia in 1648 that led to France's annexation of Alsace and Lorraine. Choucroute is obviously German in origin, but the French welcomed it with open arms.

The word *choucroute* is basically a French phonetic spelling of the German *sauerkraut,* and the French version means "cabbage crust." Any combination of pickled cabbage with meat could be considered choucroute garni (*garni* means "garnished," and the garnish for this dish is mostly meat, usually a selection of sausages, cured meats, and even some fresh pork).

To follow (most) traditions, there should be Strasbourg sausage (similar to knackwurst, with the initial *k* pronounced), Montbéliard sausage (a smoked wurst flavored with cumin, garlic, and white wine), and Frankfurt sausage (you guessed it, frankfurters). Also welcome as a choucroute garnish are smoked ham hocks or bacon.

Boiled potatoes are the starch of choice, and seasonings should include black pepper, cloves, and juniper berries—with some onions to sweeten the deal and a little white wine to brighten the flavors.

Refugees from Alsace, most notably Frédéric Bofinger (see sidebar at right) brought choucroute (and draft beer!) to Paris, where it became a staple, first of the brasseries, and then other casual restaurants.

BRASSERIE BOFINGER

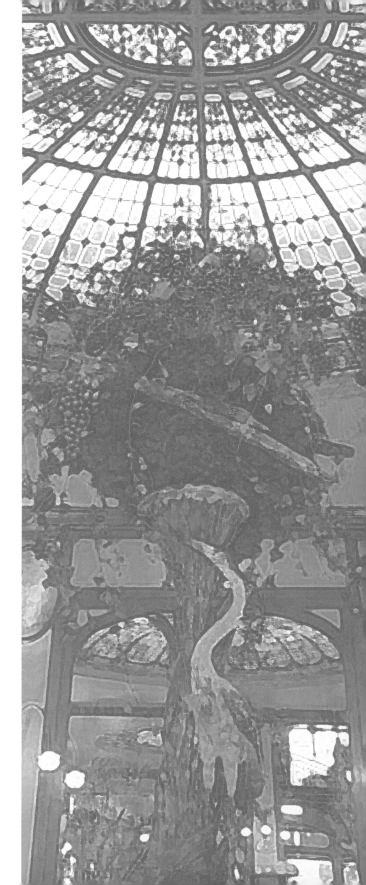

THIS IS ONE OF the most famous, and popular, casual restaurants in Paris. With a worldwide reputation, it was founded by Frédéric Bofinger, a refugee of the Franco-Prussian War. Bofinger opened a small brasserie in 1864, and his Alsatian heritage proved useful in a few ways. Fate took a hand as well, in that the scourge of phylloxera hit the vineyards of France just about the same time that the Prussian army trounced their French counterparts in Alsace. (The phylloxera louse had infested French vineyards and almost totally devastated the wine crop.)

So, Bofinger fled to Paris, where he planned to serve the local specialties of Alsace, choucroute garnis and beer. The choucroute (literally, sauerkraut) was a great casual dish, but the beer was even more important because there was almost no wine available!

Starting with the first draught draft beer ever served in Paris, Brasserie Bofinger grew to the point where they now serve more than 800 guests each day. The ubiquitous *plateau de fruits de mer* (seafood platter) has been on the menu for years, and joins other familiar characters such as onion soup and foie gras. A hundred plates of choucroute garnis each day is the norm for this Paris fixture, and it will be available when you go there. It will be the best sauerkraut you ever had. Try to get a table under the famous stained-glass ceiling in the main dining room.

Poitrine de Porc aux d'Épices *Sous-Vide*

Sous-Vide *Spiced Pork Belly*

GIVE YOURSELF SEVERAL days to prepare this dish. You'll need to allow four days for the pork to cure and one more day to prepare it "sous-vide."

SERVES 6

DRY CURE

(makes more than required for this recipe)

6 tbsp fennel seeds

6 tbsp cumin seeds

1 tbsp coriander seeds

4 tsp black peppercorns

2 pieces star anise

2 cinnamon sticks

1 tsp white peppercorns

1½ tsp cloves

1½ tsp ground coriander

3 lb pork belly

½ cup salt

¼ cup sugar

2 cups Chicken Stock*

1 cup Riesling wine

½ cup Demi-glace*

4 tbsp chopped cornichons

*For recipes and information about substitutions, see Fonds de Cuisine, page 175.

1. Begin to cure the pork 4 days before you want to serve it. To make the dry cure, blend the first 9 ingredients in a coffee grinder or blender until the mixture becomes a very fine powder. (You will only need 6 tablespoons for this recipe; store any that remains in a sealed jar or tin. Try it on other cuts of pork.)

2. Cut the pork belly into 2 pieces. Combine 6 tablespoons of the dry cure with the salt and sugar. Rub this mixture in an even layer on both sides of the meat. Keep the rest of the dry cure for another day. Cover the pork and refrigerate for 4 days.

3. Pour the chicken stock into a shallow pan or ice cube trays. Freeze until solid. This freezing facilitates easier vacuuming.

4. One day before serving, rinse the pork belly pieces and place into vacuuming bags. Add half of the chicken stock to each bag and seal using a vacuum-pack machine. Place the bags in a large saucepan, cover with water and heat to 190 to 200°F. Cover the pan and cook for 6½ to 7 hours. Check the temperature with a thermometer and occasionally move the bags around during cooking. Remove the bags and cool them to room temperature. Refrigerate overnight.

5. When you're ready for the final preparations, preheat the oven to 475°F. Remove the pork belly from the bags, reserve the liquid, and sear the meat in a pan over high heat until

colored on both sides. Cook in the oven until golden and crisp on both sides, 30 to 40 minutes. Carve into ¼-inch-thick slices. In a small saucepot, reduce the Riesling wine over high heat by half. Add the reserved liquid from the vacuum-packed bags, the demi-glace, and cornichons, and reduce to a saucy consistency.

6. To serve, place the pork on a heated platter or plates. Pour the sauce over the pork and serve.

◇◇◇◇◇◇◇◇◇◇◇◇◇◇◇◇◇◇◇◇◇◇◇◇◇◇◇◇

BEVERAGE: PINOT NOIR OR GAMAY

A lighter-style Pinot Noir or Gamay works very nicely with this dish or one of the *cru* villages of Beaujolais.

◇◇

TOM VALENTI'S LAMB SHANKS

SOME CHEFS MAKE TALL FOOD. Some do fusion, and some are rooted firmly to the classics. Tom Valenti is capable of each one of these, yet is best known for making food that brims with rich, complex, comforting flavor. The best chefs simply make food that tastes great, no matter what else their philosophy.

Tom grew up in an Italian-American home in Ithaca, New York, gaining an innate understanding of food from his grandmother. After working in a French restaurant during high school, he worked for the legendary chef Guy Savoy, first in New York (Westchester County), and then in France. Back in New York City, Tom became a sous-chef at the seminal downtown restaurant, Gotham Bar and Grill, under chef Alfred Portale.

New Yorkers really took notice, though, when Tom became the first executive chef at a small but important restaurant called Alison on Dominick. The restaurant was out of the way, hard to find, distant from all subway lines, yet busy all the time. Almost literally a jewel box—tiny and lined with navy blue velvet curtains—the food was remarkable; elegant, hearty, refined, gutsy. Tom got people to eat things that they might normally avoid like fried, impossibly small eels served as an *amuse-bouche*. Even more improbable, he became famous for his Braised Lamb Shanks with White Bean Purée. With the luscious meat falling off the bone into the soft cushion of rich bean purée, it was the kind of dish you would find yourself daydreaming about while waiting for the F train.

The lamb shanks garnered citywide attention, and word got out that this was the best new comfort food to be found in a fine dining restaurant. Newspapers, magazines, and dining guides all mentioned this dish;

so other chefs followed suit. The weird part is that the demand for lamb shanks, which had always been cheap and considered somewhat low-class, increased so much that their price more than doubled. It has been said that Tom Valenti single-handedly raised the wholesale price of lamb shanks in New York City.

Tom is an old friend, and has been gracious enough to allow me to include his famous recipe in this book. The shanks are perfect, the bean purée rich and reassuringly earthy. I was intrigued by the use of distilled white vinegar in the dish, something one is more likely to use to clean windows than put in a braise. Tom explained it this way:

"At first, I was using wine to braise with, but noticed that the acidity wasn't quite there to balance the richness of the rich meat flavor. I tried different vinegars, but in the amounts that were necessary, they started getting expensive. I figured that what I needed was just the acid, so I went for the simplest and most affordable version, distilled white vinegar. Thing is, we were now missing out on some flavor, so I added the anchovies to fill in the gaps. It's a combination that I continue to use, because it gives a great balance of richness of flavor with brightness—and it's affordable!"

This is a great example of how a *thinking* chef works. Revere and use the classic methods, but never stop questioning and experimenting. The best part of this scientific method is that the research leads to tangible, and edible, data.

Braised Lamb Shanks

with White Bean Purée

THIS DISH, AS it is served at Chef Valenti's restaurant, is the very essence of comfort food, but it's presentation is very dramatic. The meat is literally falling off the shank bone into the sumptuous, velvety purée of white beans.

If you plan to serve the white bean purée as an accompaniment to the lamb shanks, remember that you need to plan on soaking the dry beans overnight, or use the alternate quick soak method described on page 127.

SERVES 6 AS A MAIN COURSE

6 lamb foreshanks (meatier than hindshanks)

Coarse salt and freshly ground black pepper as needed

½ cup plus 3 tbsp olive oil, divided use

2 ribs celery, chopped

1 carrot, chopped

1 large Spanish onion, chopped

½ cup tomato paste

5 sprigs thyme

1 bay leaf

1 tbsp black peppercorns

3 anchovy fillets

1 whole head garlic, cut in half horizontally

2 cups red wine

1 cup dry white wine

⅓ cup distilled white vinegar

1 tsp sugar

2 cups Veal Stock* or 1 cup Demi-glace*

2 cups Chicken Stock*

White Bean Puree (recipe follows)

*For recipes and information about substitutions, see Fonds de Cuisine, page 175.

1. Preheat the oven to 325°F. Season the lamb shanks liberally with salt and pepper. With a sharp knife, cut about 1 inch from the bottom (narrow end) of each shank bone down to the bone and all the way around; this will help expose the bones while cooking. Set them aside.

2. Heat 3 tablespoons of the oil in a Dutch oven or flameproof casserole over medium-high heat. Add the shanks, a few at a time, and cook until colored on all sides. Transfer the shanks to a plate and keep warm.

3. If necessary, add a bit more of the oil to the casserole. Add the celery, carrot, and onion to the casserole and cook until they're very soft, 8 to 10 minutes. Add the tomato paste and cook 1 to 2 minutes until it turns a russet color and smells sweet. Add the thyme, bay leaf, peppercorns, an-chovies, and garlic, and cook another 2 to 3 minutes to release their flavors.

4. Add the red and white wine, vinegar, and sugar. Bring the mixture to a boil. Lower the heat to medium and add the veal stock (or demi-glace) and chicken stock. Continue to cook over medium heat while you brown the shanks.

5. Return the shanks to the casserole along with any juices they have released. Cover the pot and place in the oven. (If your shanks won't fit in your casserole, transfer the shanks to a roasting pan and pour the stock mixture on top. Cover with aluminum foil.) Remove the cover (or the foil) from the casserole after 1 hour and continue to braise for another 3 hours, turning the shanks over every half hour until the meat is very soft. Remove the shanks from the braising liquid and strain the liquid. Skim any fat that rises to the surface and use the liquid as a sauce.

6. Serve the shanks on a pool of hot white bean purée with the sauce.

◇◇◇◇◇◇◇◇◇◇◇◇◇

BEVERAGE: CAHORS

While red Bordeaux is often paired with elegant lamb dishes, this more rustic dish can be paired with a more rustic wine. So, east and just south of Bordeaux is a region that produces a big wine (some-times called the 'Black Wine of Cahors' based on the Malbec grape, here called *Auxerrois*.

White Bean Purée

MAKES ABOUT 3 CUPS

1½ cups dried great Northern beans

1 medium white onion, cut into small dice

1 medium carrot, cut into small dice

1 celery rib, cut into small dice

1 garlic clove, smashed

2 sprigs thyme

1 bay leaf

5 to 6 cups (approximately) Chicken Stock or water,
  more if needed for cooking beans*

TO FINISH THE PURÉE:

⅓ cup heavy cream

1 tsp fresh thyme leaves

1 garlic clove, minced

Coarse salt and pepper as needed

Few drops extra-virgin olive oil

*For recipes and information about substitutions,
see Fonds de Cuisine, page 175.

1. Soak the beans overnight or, alternately, use the quick soak method: Place them in a pot, cover with water, and bring to a boil over high heat. Remove the pot from the heat and set aside, covered, for 1 hour.

2. Drain the beans and transfer them to a 2-quart saucepan with the onion, carrot, celery, smashed garlic, thyme sprigs, bay leaf, and five cups of the stock.

3. Season the beans with salt and pepper and bring them to a boil over high heat. Immediately lower the heat and simmer for 90 minutes, or until very tender. If the mixture becomes dry, add some additional stock or water. Drain the beans in a colander. Pick out and discard the thyme sprigs and bay leaf.

4. To finish the purée, warm the beans and vegetables in a large sauté pan over medium heat. Add the cream, thyme leaves, and minced garlic to the pan and season with salt and pepper. Raise the heat to high, bring the beans to a boil, and then lower to a simmer. Cook until the cream is reduced and almost dry on the beans and the beans are heated through, 4 to 5 minutes.

5. Transfer the bean mixture to a food processor and process until it's smooth, adding a few drops of oil until the purée glistens a bit. Adjust the seasoning with salt and pepper as needed and pulse it to just combine.

6. If making in advance, cool the purée in a large stainless steel bowl and set it in another bowl filled with ice water. Transfer the beans to an airtight container after they've cooled and refrigerate them for up to 2 days. To warm the purée before you serve it, put a thin layer of water in a sauce pan, bring the bean purée to room temperature, then warm it in a pan over medium-high heat.

Potée de Campagne

Country-Style Lamb Stew

THIS HEARTY LAMB stew is perfect for a cold winter's day and like all stews, it is very accommodating with regard to serving. Making the stew up to 3 days in advance and reheating will not only make a busy life simpler, it will enhance the flavor. It's absolutely delicious!

SERVES 6

3 tbsp clarified butter*

3 lb lamb shoulder, cut into 1½-inch cubes

Salt and pepper as needed

2 tbsp all-purpose flour

2 cups chopped shallots

2 tbsp tomato paste

2 cups dry white wine

1 cup crushed tomatoes

5 cups Lamb or Veal Stock*

1 sachet* plus ½ head of garlic

18 small fingerling or new potatoes

1 cup parsnips, peeled and cut into batons

1 cup white turnips, peeled and cut into batons

1 cup rutabaga, peeled and cut into batons

2¾ cups baby carrots, peeled

2 tbsp unsalted butter

½ tsp sugar

18 haricot verts or green beans

6 tbsp shelled fresh peas

1 tbsp chopped parsley

*For recipes and information about substitutions, see Fonds de Cuisine, page 175.

1. Heat the clarified butter in a large, heavy, thick-bottomed pan. Place the lamb in a bowl and season it with salt and pepper. Sprinkle the flour over the lamb and toss until the meat is thoroughly coated. Sear the lamb in the butter over high heat, a few pieces at a time, until it's browned. Remove it from the pan and reserve; continue this process until all the lamb has been seared.

2. Lower the heat to medium and add the shallots. Lightly brown the shallots, about 3 minutes, and add the tomato paste. Cook for 5 minutes, stirring frequently. Add the white wine and reduce it by half. Return the lamb to the pan and add the crushed tomatoes and stock, along with the sachet with the garlic. Stir well. Bring the mix to a boil, then turn the heat down to maintain a slow simmer. Cover the pan with a lid.

3. Simmer the stew for 1 hour, then remove the lid and continue to cook for another 30 to 45 minutes. The flavor of the sauce will strengthen as the liquid evaporates. Taste the sauce when the meat is tender. If the sauce does not have enough flavor and does not lightly coat the back of a spoon, then strain off half of the sauce and reduce it to taste. Return the reduced sauce to the stew, season it with salt and pepper, and keep

it warm (or you can cool the stew and save it to reheat on another day.)

4. Cook the potatoes in salted water on medium heat until tender, about 20 minutes. Drain the potatoes and keep them warm until ready to serve the stew.

5. Combine the parsnips, turnips, rutabagas, carrots, butter, and sugar in a small pan. Add water to just below the level of the vegetables. Add a pinch of salt and bring to the boil over high heat. Boil the vegetables rapidly until they're cooked, 10 to 15 minutes, and then add the beans and peas. Continue to reduce the liquid until a syrup forms and the vegetables are lightly coated. Toss the vegetables in the glaze and sprinkle them with chopped parsley.

6. Serve the stew garnished with the glazed vegetables, and potatoes served as a side.

◇◇◇◇◇◇◇

BEVERAGE:

Good red Burgundy is perfect with this hearty dish, but you could also enjoy a young New World Cabernet Sauvignon.

Gigot d'Agneau avec Pommes de Terre Boulangère

Roast Leg of Lamb with Baked Potatoes and Onions

SERVES 6

3 lb leg of lamb, bone in

1 garlic clove, very thinly sliced

4 sprigs thyme, divided use

Salt and pepper as needed

½ cup lard, melted

1 recipe Pommes Boulangère (page 81)

1¾ cup large-dice onion

¾ cup large-dice peeled celery

⅔ cup peeled, large-dice carrots

⅔ cup peeled, large-dice parsnips

1 tsp tomato paste

1 bay leaf

½ cup white wine

4 cups Lamb or Veal Stock*

*For recipes and information about substitutions, see Fonds de Cuisine, page 175.

1. Preheat the oven to 400°F. Pierce the meat with a paring knife just beneath the skin and push about half of the garlic slices into the incisions, along with 2 sprigs of the thyme torn into pieces. Rub the skin with enough salt and pepper to lightly coat. Place the lamb on a rack in a roasting pan and pour the lard drippings over it. When the potatoes have been cooking for 30

minutes, place the lamb into the oven and cook for 30 minutes, and then turn the oven down to 350°F. Continue to roast the lamb for another 30 minutes, basting the meat every 15 minutes.

3. Remove the pan from the oven and place the diced vegetables and remaining sliced garlic under the roasting rack. The juices from the meat will drip onto your vegetables and give them a wonderful flavor. Return the lamb and vegetables to the oven and roast for an additional 30 minutes, by which time the vegetables will have started to take on a golden brown color. Turn the vegetables, so they cook evenly. Reduce the heat to 300°F for the last 15 to 20 minutes of cooking; the lamb should be finished to your liking at this point. (See page 175 for more about determining the doneness of meats.)

4. Remove the lamb from the oven and transfer to a platter. Keep warm while preparing the gravy. (This also lets the meat "rest" before you carve it; you'll find that meats allowed to rest before carving slice better and are much juicier.)

5. To make the gravy, pour off the drippings from the roasting pan and save it in the refrigerator to baste your next roast. Leave a little of the fat with the vegetables and all of the brown fond from the roast in the pan, put it directly over the burner (medium heat) and fry the vegetables for

about 4 minutes, or until they are lightly caramelized. Add the tomato paste and cook about 2 more minutes, stirring frequently. Be careful not to burn the vegetables or tomato paste.

6. Add the remaining 2 sprigs of thyme and the bay leaf. Add the wine and reduce the gravy over medium heat until it's almost dry, about 3 minutes. Add the stock and reduce it until the sauce lightly coats the roasted vegetables, about 20 minutes. Any juices that have come from the lamb resting on the plate can be added to the sauce to improve its flavor. Season the sauce with salt and pepper. You may strain the sauce at this point or leave the vegetables in.

7. Place the potatoes back in the oven to warm them up, if needed. Remove them when warmed and sprinkle with the chopped parsley. Place the lamb on top of the potatoes to carve. To serve, arrange the potatoes in a semicircle around the outside of the plate, place the carved lamb in the center, and finish the dish with sauce.

◇◇◇◇◇◇◇◇◇◇◇◇

ROASTING TIME:

25 minutes per pound, plus 25 minutes.

◇◇◇◇◇◇◇◇◇◇◇◇◇◇◇◇◇◇◇◇◇◇◇◇◇◇

BEVERAGE: BORDEAUX ROUGE

This is an intentionally broad wine recommendation. Because a roast leg of lamb can be served both as a simple family dinner, or as the centerpiece of a special event, the wine can be either a *cru bourgeois* from the bargain bin of French wines, or a first growth from the Haut-Médoc. The whole price range is available to you, from $3.99 to $399, and the lamb will taste delicious with any of them.

Pot-au-Feu

Pot on Fire

THIS DISH IS elemental to the French cuisine and, therefore, an integral part of every French person's life. The "pot on fire" is filled with a variety of ingredients, depending on the region. There is always a tough cut of meat (usually beef) and a combination of aromatic and eventually edible vegetables, cooked with very few spices (usually just salt, pepper, and a few cloves).

The concept had been around for centuries under different names, but the first written recipes for *pot-au-feu* appeared in the mid 1800s, one of which was written by Antonin Carême, one of France's most acclaimed chefs and prolific food writers. It is unfortunate that the popularity of this dish seems to be waning amongst home cooks in France, mostly because of the time it takes to prepare. Ironically, the dish is quite simple to prepare—it just takes time to put the ingredients together and needs to be watched.

You may want to plan on preparing this over the course of two days: Make the broth the first day, and do final cooking the day you'll be serving it. It's easier to remove the fat from the broth when it has solidified during refrigeration.

SERVES 8 AS A MAIN COURSE (WITH LEFTOVERS)

2 lb beef short ribs, cut into serving-sized pieces, fat trimmed

2 lb beef brisket

2 lb beef chuck roast, tied

3 lb veal bones (choose meaty knuckle bones)

1 lb beef rib bones (optional)

3 to 4 lb chicken, quartered

4 garlic cloves

2 medium yellow onions

1 leek, trimmed but left whole

2 large carrots

*1 sachet**

Salt as needed

SERVING VEGETABLES

4 large carrots, cut into large dice

1 large celeriac, cut into large dice

2 parsnips, cut into large dice

2 white turnips, cut into large dice

4 large waxy potatoes, cut into large dice

3 leeks, trimmed and cut into 1-inch pieces

*For recipes and information about substitutions, see Fonds de Cuisine, page 175.

1. To blanch the meats, place the meat, bones, and chicken in a casserole or stockpot large enough to hold them comfortably. Cover with cold water and bring to a boil, then lower to a low simmer, with bubbles occasionally breaking the surface. (This blanching steps give the meats

a chance to "throw off" the impurities that might cloud the stock. It produces a rich, sparkling, deep golden broth.)

2. When gray foam forms on the surface, after about 10 minutes of simmering, skim it off and remove the meat, holding it aside. Drain the water and clean out the pot. Put the meat back in the pot and add fresh water to cover by 2 inches. Heat again to a boil, and then lower to a simmer. Add the garlic, onions, leek, carrots, and the sachet to the pot. Cook at a low simmer. If any scum forms on the surface (it should be white now), skim it off.

3. As the meats reach the point when a serving fork pulls out easily (more important than how easily it goes in), remove them from the broth and hold aside. The chicken will become fork-tender after about 45 minutes, the rest of the meats after about an hour.

4. When all the meats have been removed, strain the broth through cheesecloth or a fine-mesh strainer. If you are cooking over the course of 2 days, refrigerate the broth and meats in separate covered containers, along with the raw, diced vegetables. If you are forging ahead, keep the broth above 140°F and remove as much fat as you can from its surface.

5. The next day, remove the congealed fat from the surface of the broth. Return the broth and meat to a large stockpot and turn the heat to high. Bring to a boil, then lower to a simmer and add the raw vegetables. When the meat is heated through and the vegetables are cooked, you're ready to serve.

Adding garnishes that lend texture and a punch of flavor makes this dish into something far more than you ever thought a meal of boiled meats and broth could be. Choose from among the following options:

Sauce Raifort (see page 181)

Toasted baguette slices with Gruyère melted on top to float in the broth

Dijon mustard

Cornichons

This dish is best when served in two courses. Start with the soup: Ladle some broth into soup bowls and top with the cheesy croutons and some chopped parsley. (Remember to put at least 1 cup of broth aside to moisten the meats in the second course.)

For the second course, cut the meat into serving pieces, then arrange the meat and vegetables on a platter. Moisten the meat and vegetables with the reserved broth and serve with the other garnishes.

A small bowl of coarse salt is another important element when you serve a true pot-au-feu. A great choice would be fleur de sel, a hand-harvested sea salt produced along the coast of Brittany. The name means "flower of salt" and the grains have a grayish color from the minerals that occur naturally in the salt—and which give it a unique savor.

Blanquette de Veau

White Veal Stew

VEAL BREAST HAS the perfect combination of meat, fat, and gelatin, which provides for the succulent richness of this peasant dish. Like so many other cheap cuts, this is about getting the most out of the least.

SERVES 6

2½ lb veal breast, cut into 1-inch dice

1 medium carrot, peeled

1 small onion, peeled

24 pearl onions, peeled

1 bouquet garni*

Salt and white pepper as needed

1 tbsp plus 1 tsp unsalted butter, divided use

3 tbsp all-purpose flour

1¼ cups white mushrooms, wiped clean

¼ cup dry white wine

2 tbsp water

Juice of ½ lemon

¼ cup clarified butter*

6 heart-shaped croûtes

2 large egg yolks

½ cup heavy cream

1 tbsp chopped parsley

*For recipes and information about substitutions, see Fonds de Cuisine, page 175.

1. Blanch the veal in boiling water for 30 seconds. Skim, drain the veal, and discard the water. Place the veal into a large saucepan and barely cover with cold water. Bring it to the boil and skim again. Add the carrot, whole onion, pearl onions, and bouquet garni. Reduce the heat, cover with a lid, and simmer gently until the meat is tender, 1 to 1½ hours. Remove and discard the carrot, whole onion, and bouquet garni.

2. Strain the cooking liquid into a medium saucepan and reduce it by one third, or until you have one pint remaining. Season the meat and pearl onions as needed with salt and pepper. Place into the serving dish.

3. To make 1 pint of velouté, melt 1 tablespoon of the butter in a medium pan over medium heat and add the flour; mix it thoroughly. Take the mix off the heat and gradually add the cooking liquid by degrees, mixing it well and boiling the sauce between additions. Simmer the sauce for 20 minutes over very low heat, or until thickened and smooth.

4. Meanwhile in a small pan, cook the mushrooms in the white wine, water, 1 teaspoon of lemon juice, and the remaining 1 teaspoon of the butter until they're just tender, about 2 minutes. Remove the mushrooms and add them to the meat and pearl onions; continue to keep the food warm. Reduce the mushroom liquid along

with any juices that have accumulated in the serving dish until it's syrupy, and pour it into the velouté.

5. Heat the clarified butter in a medium skillet and fry the heart-shaped croûtes on medium heat until they're golden on both sides; drain them on paper towels and keep them warm.

6. Mix the egg yolks and cream together in a medium bowl to make a liaison. Take the simmering velouté off the heat and add ½ cup of the sauce to the liaison. Mix it thoroughly and immediately pour it back into the hot velouté, whisking thoroughly. Do not return the sauce to the heat at this point. Season the sauce as needed with salt and pepper, then strain it and pour it over the meat, mushrooms, and pearl onions. Garnish the meat with the croûtes and sprinkle it with parsley to serve.

◇◇◇◇◇◇◇◇◇◇◇◇◇◇◇◇◇◇◇◇◇◇◇◇◇◇◇◇◇◇

BEVERAGE: AUXEY-DURESSES BLANC OR CÔTE DE BEAUNE-VILLAGES BLANC

Classy, rich veal stew. Classy, rich white wine. But, this is a stew, after all, so there's no need to break the bank. Auxey-Duresses is right next to the village of Meursault, and produces wines similar to those of its neighbor, though a little less rich (in more ways than one).

Boeuf Bourguignon

Beef Stew with Red Wine

THE BURGUNDIANS FAVOR their famous Charolais beef cattle for this regional dish. This makes perfect sense because the breed holds AOC and is reared under strict guidelines for feeding and living conditions (see sidebar). This pursuit of excellence produces beef with superior flavor and taste. If you have a similar passion for excellence but don't have access to Charolais, then seek out your local producers of grass-fed beef and do your cooking justice.

SERVES 6 TO 8

3 lb shin or neck of beef, cut into 2-inch cubes

4 cups mirepoix (2 cups chopped onions, 2 cups chopped carrots)

2 bottles Côtes du Rhône or red Burgundy

10 oz bacon lardons*

24 pearl onions, peeled

3 ½ cups small white mushrooms, wiped clean

½ cup clarified butter*

Salt and pepper as needed

6 garlic cloves, chopped

1 tbsp tomato paste (optional)

½ cup toasted flour, sifted*

1 large bouquet garni*

1 tsp sugar

8 heart-shaped croutons, sautéed in unsalted butter

1 tsp chopped parsley

*For recipes and information about substitutions, see Fonds de Cuisine, page 175.

1. Marinate the beef with the mirepoix and wine for 24 hours in the refrigerator.

2. The next day, preheat the oven to 300°F. Cook the bacon lardons in a large, heavy cast-iron pan until golden, yet not too crisp, about 5 minutes. Remove, cool, and set them aside. Sear the pearl onions in the same pan used for the lardons over medium heat until they have good color, about 5 minutes. Remove, cool, and set them aside. Sear the mushrooms over medium heat until they're browned, about 5 minutes. Store them with the bacon lardons.

3. Remove the meat from the marinade, and set the marinade aside. In a large, heavy cast-iron pan, sear the meat in the clarified butter, cooking just a few pieces at a time; don't add too much meat at one time because that will cause the pan to cool and the meat to boil in its own juices. Sear until the meat becomes a good brown color (in this case it will be purplish-brown because of the wine). Season the meat as needed with salt and pepper. Remove the meat from the pan with a slotted spoon and set it aside on a plate. You should be left with about 2 tablespoons of fat in the pan; if necessary, add a bit more more clarified butter.

4. Add the garlic and tomato paste (if using) to

the pan and cook over low heat for 2 minutes, stirring constantly. Return the meat and any accumulated juices to the pan, stirring well to release the caramelized juices created from searing it.

5. Take the pan off the heat and add the sifted toasted flour to the meat, stirring thoroughly. Pour in the wine marinade and again mix thoroughly to fully distribute the flour for even thickening. Return the pan to medium heat and bring to a boil; add the bouquet garni and sugar.

6. Cover the pan with a lid that fits well—this will prevent the meat from drying out during the 3 hours of cooking. Bake in the oven; check every hour to make sure it's simmering gently. If it's becoming dry, add a little water to moisten it but be careful not to dilute the flavor. After 2½ hours of cooking, add the seared onions, mushrooms, and bacon.

7. After it has cooked for 3 hours, remove from the oven, skim off the fat, and gently reduce the sauce on the stove over medium heat with the lid off the pan until the sauce has the flavor and consistency you prefer.

8. Transfer the stew to a serving dish and garnish with croutons and parsley. Serve with boiled or mashed potatoes.

◇◇◇◇◇◇◇◇◇◇◇◇◇◇◇◇◇◇◇◇◇◇◇◇◇◇◇◇

BEVERAGE: BOURGOGNE ROUGE

To be authentic, you should use red Burgundy in the braising liquid. To connect the dish with its vinous partner, drink the same. Remember, though, that you don't have to use the same wine for both. The subtleties of a fine wine are lost in a long braise, but not on your palate.

APPELLATION D'ORIGIN CONTRÔLÉE (AOC)

THE FRENCH HAVE BEEN at the forefront when it comes to protecting the quality and character of regional products. As early as the 15th century, a parliamentary decree established specific standards for Rouquefort.

AOC rules govern agriculture products by carefully defining their geographic location. The products must come from approved producers within the region, and they must meet strict standards of production in order to put AOC on their labels. Since 1990, the original 1935 laws established to govern the production of wine have been extended to other agricultural goods including cheeses, meats, and poultry.

Many other countries have similar laws. You'll even see the term AOC on products made in this country, as a way of indicating that they come from a specific location, even though we have no official AOC in the United States. What it means to us is that the flavors of the food or wine will reflect the sun and soil that produced it.

Steak Frîtes

Pan-Fried Steak

HOW CAN THIS be a French dish? Meat and fried potatoes are an American icon. Yet, somehow, this specific way of putting them together seems, somehow, Gallic. The key to the steaks is the touch of butter as they cook and again in the sauce, and the secret of great fries is, of course, the double cooking. You'll never want fast-food fries again. Oh, and maybe that last bit of butter, swirled in at the last minute. Maybe that's what makes if French.

The best pan for the steaks is a seasoned cast-iron skillet. Its heat retention properties make it a great pan to get the browned crust on the steaks while cooking them to just the right temperature inside. As for the potatoes, a heavy 4-quart saucepan with tall sides will work if you don't have an electric French fry maker.

SERVES 4 TO 6 AS A MAIN COURSE

Pommes Frîtes (page 71)

4 to 6 beef steaks, boneless rib or strip (½ lb
    per portion, at least ½ inch thick)

Salt and coarsely ground black pepper as needed

4 tbsp salted butter, divided use

1 tsp peanut oil

½ cup water, or Chicken or Beef Stock (page 181)

1. Prepare the pommes frîtes as directed on page 71 up through the blanching step. Hold them at room temperature until you are ready to prepare the steaks.

2. Remove all of the fat from the sides of the steaks. It's the interior marbling of the fat that gives the steaks their juiciness, so removing it from the sides won't diminish the flavor. Heat a large, well-seasoned cast iron pan on high until it's hot but not smoking. Season the steaks on both sides with plenty of salt and pepper. Put them in the pan with no added fat. There will be quite a bit of smoke.

3. After the first side is browned, about 1 minute, turn the steaks over, turn the heat down to medium and add 2 tablespoons of the butter and the peanut oil to the pan. The oil doesn't actually lower the smoking point of the butter, but it does help keep it from burning as easily.

4. Heat the oil in the fryer up to 360°F, and cook the blanched fries in batches until they're crisp and golden. Drain them on fresh paper towels, and season liberally with salt and pepper. Keep warm in a 200°F oven.

5. When juice seeps to the surface of the steaks,

after 1 or 2 minutes, remove them from the pan and keep covered on a warm plate. They'll be close to medium-rare, or *à point*.

6. Turn the heat to low under the sauté pan and deglaze with the water or stock, scraping up the browned bits. Reduce the liquid by half, about 4 minutes, and pour in the accumulated juices from the steaks. Montè au beurre (whisk in) the remaining 2 tablespoons of butter and pour the resulting sauce over the steaks. Serve each guest their own steak with a pile of fries.

◇◇◇◇◇◇◇◇◇◇◇◇◇◇◇◇◇◇◇◇◇◇◇◇◇◇◇◇

BEVERAGE: RED WINE OR AMBER BEER

Let's not overthink this one. Steak, french fries, good red wine, good amber beer. Don't think; just eat and drink.

Carbonnade à la Flamande

Flemish-Style Braised Beef and Onions

THE VINEGAR ADDED at the end of the cooking should brighten the flavors without being obvious—add just a little at a time and stop before you really notice it. Serve the stew with mashed potatoes and a simple green vegetable. This will put the comfort-food receptors into overload.

SERVES 6 TO 8 AS A MAIN COURSE

3 lb chuck or bottom round beef

1 tsp salt

½ tsp pepper

2 tbsp olive oil

2 lb yellow onions, thinly sliced

2 garlic cloves, minced

1 tbsp all-purpose flour

1½ cups dark beer

2 sprigs fresh or 1 tsp dried thyme

2 bay leaves

1 tbsp malt vinegar

NOTE: The beer you use should be malty, sweet, and brown (or amber) and relatively low on hops. Bitterness in the beer will concentrate as the gravy reduces and can become unpleasant.

1. Cut the beef into 1-inch slices. Season the meat with salt and pepper, and brown it on all sides over medium-high heat; set aside. Do this in batches if the pan is not large enough to hold all the meat at once without crowding the pan.

2. Heat the oil in a casserole on medium heat and add the onions. Stir occasionally and let them soften, about 5 minutes. Add the garlic and wait until the raw smell goes away, 2 to 3 minutes. Add the flour, stir it in, and cook until the flour no longer smells raw, about 2 minutes.

3. Return the meat to the casserole and add the beer and herbs. Give it all a big stir, bring it to a boil then lower to a simmer. Allow it to simmer gently, partially covered, for about 3 hours. The meat should be fork-tender when it's done.

4. If the liquid is too thin, pour the entire contents of the casserole through a strainer or colander and return the liquid to the casserole. Reduce until it's syrupy and then return the meat and onions to the casserole to heat them through. Check for final seasoning and adjust with salt, pepper, and vinegar.

◇◇◇◇◇◇◇◇◇◇◇◇◇◇◇◇◇◇◇◇◇◇◇◇◇◇◇◇◇◇◇◇

BEVERAGE: BEER, ESPECIALLY A BELGIAN TRIPEL

Belgian tripel is brewed in a process that calls for three times the malt used in a Trappist Simple ale. This gives the tripel a much greater percentage of alcohol, up to around 10% alcohol by volume. That, plus the fact that the malt produces a somewhat sweeter beer, means that tripel is a great choice when you need a beer with enough body to keep up with the stew.

Steak au Poivre Verts

Steak with Green Peppercorns

WHEN MANY PEOPLE think of steak au poivre they think of a steak covered with cracked black peppercorns. Since that dish is just a variation on Steak Frîtes (see page 140), we've provided this recipe for steak in a green peppercorn sauce. It's a bit more luxurious, and because it's coated with sauce, all exterior fat should be removed from the steaks so you won't inadvertently end up with a mouthful of gristle. Also, while fried potatoes are fine with this, you may want to try mashed potatoes because they absorb the sauce and meat juices—yum. Sautéed spinach is another fine accompaniment.

The cut of meat you use is up to you. In descending order of flavor, but increasing levels of tenderness would be hanger steak, top sirloin, New York strip, and tenderloin. While we prefer the first three for taste, the tenderloin is a more luxurious choice, and the delicious sauce compensates for its lack of flavor.

SERVES 4 AS A MAIN COURSE

4 hanger, top sirloin, New York strip, or tenderloin steaks (5 to 6 oz per portion)

Salt and pepper as needed

1 tsp peanut or grapeseed oil

1 tbsp unsalted butter

2 tbsp minced shallots

2 tbsp green peppercorns, rinsed

1 tbsp cognac or dry brandy

½ cup Beef Broth* or water

½ cup Demi-glace*

½ cup heavy cream

*For recipes and information about substitutions, see Fonds de Cuisine, page 175.

1. Dry the steaks with paper towels and season well on both sides with salt and pepper.

2. Heat a large sauté pan until very hot, then add the oil. (Both peanut oil and grapeseed oil have high smoking points, making them ideal for frying at very high temperatures.)

3. Sear the steaks on both sides, but remove them from the pan when they're still slightly undercooked, 1 to 2 minutes each side (remove the steaks when they're still rare if you want the final cooking temperature to be medium-rare). Cover and hold on the side (on a dinner plate with another dinner plate inverted on top works well).

4. Lower the heat to medium and add the butter and shallots. Stir the shallots occasionally to prevent burning, and when translucent, after 2 to 3 minutes, add the green peppercorns. Lightly crush the peppercorns with the back of a wooden spoon or dinner fork to keep them from popping, and to release more of their flavor.

5. With the pan off the heat, add the cognac or brandy. Be careful—it may flame up. Add the broth or water and scrape up the browned bits from the pan. Return it to the heat and allow the

liquid to reduce by half. (Flaming the brandy can be exciting, but is a bit dangerous.)

6. Add the demi-glace and cream; stir to combine and return the steaks to the pan, along with their accumulated juices. When the steaks have been coated with sauce and warmed through, put them on serving plates (slicing them before plating is a more elegant *soignée* option). Check the sauce for seasoning and a heavy cream consistency; adjust as needed with salt and pepper, pour it over the steaks and serve.

◇◇◇◇

NOTE:

A cast-iron fry pan works best for this. Grilling the steaks and making a separate sauce will work, but you'll lose all the great flavor from the fond that's achieved by searing the steaks in the same pan that the sauce is made in. In that case, do not heavily sear the steaks because the fond will almost certainly be burned, and unusable for the sauce.

◇◇◇◇◇◇◇◇◇◇◇◇◇◇◇◇◇◇

BEVERAGE: SAINT ÉMILION

The wines of Bordeaux's Right Bank are blends dominated by Merlot and Cabernet Franc, and the wines usually show a bit more richness and fruit than their friends from the Left Bank in the Médoc. These flavor characteristics will do well with both the pepper and cream in this dish.

CHAPTER SIX

ENTREMETS

Desserts

Now, MOST CASUAL RESTAURANTS don't have pastry chefs. That is to say, they don't have a person who *only makes desserts.* That post is usually reserved for more highfalutin' places that also have someone who does nothing but make little canapés for guests when they first sit down.

Because it is not likely that a bistro or brasserie, or even a family-style American restaurant, will have someone to make fancy desserts, there is a category of after-dinner sweets that we in the business refer to as "restaurant" or "cook's desserts." They tend to be rather simple to prepare while in the midst of other prep work, and often have a welcomed rusticity that matches the demeanor of the casual restaurant.

Perhaps the most representative of these desserts is Tarte Tatin (page 159)—caramelized apples on a puff pastry or pie crust, served warm with a scoop of vanilla ice cream or a dollop of whipped cream—few can completely ignore its charms. It is also incredibly easy to make—low effort for high impact at the table. Other cook's desserts include Profiteroles (page 152), which are properly filled with pastry cream, not ice cream, Crème Caramel (page 167), Crème Brûlée (page 166), Tarte au Citron (page 155), and a host of others. Perhaps the best example of an American cook's dessert is pie. Who doesn't like pie? The best thing is that pie as well as the fancier sounding desserts mentioned above are all easy to make. Really. Go ahead, make some dessert!

Dessert Wines

DESSERT WINE is not always what people think it is. Sure, it's sweet, and is usually served after dinner. In fact, many wine professionals prefer the term "sweet wine" instead of dessert wine. These wines are drunk as a dessert, not necessarily with a dessert.

The range of flavors and intensities of various dessert wines are hard to pin down or put into simple categories. Moscato d'Asti is a delicate, floral, low-alcohol sparkling wine, while vintage Port is dark, thick, and rich with more than twice the alcohol of the Moscato. There are myriad flavors and degrees of body in-between.

You can serve a dessert wine in one of three ways: by itself, with simple desserts, especially some of the desserts featured in this chapter, or with cheese.

There are some classic cheese and dessert wine pairings. Two of the most famous blue cheeses – Roquefort and Stilton – have equally famous classic sweet-wine partners: Sauternes for Roquefort and Vintage Port for Stilton.

If you are serving a dessert that is very complex or very rich, our best piece of advice is to avoid pitting a dessert wine against it. And whatever wine you choose to serve with dessert, make sure the wine has enough substance to stand up to the flavors and textures of your dessert.

BEIGNETS

Deep-Fried Chou Pastries

⸙

A FRITURE *IS* a pot used to fry foods on the stovetop. Choose a deep pot with an opening wide enough to permit you to add foods to the oil without resorting to dropping them. The technique we use here will keep your fingers out of the way of the hot oil.

SERVES 6, MAKES 12 PIECES

Canola oil for frying (enough to fill the pan no more than ⅓ full)

1 lb Pâte à Chou*

¼ cup vegetable oil, for brushing

Powdered sugar, for dusting

1½ cups Sauce d'Abricot*

*For recipes and information about substitutions, see Fonds de Cuisine, page 175.

1. Pour the oil into a medium thick-bottomed pan (remember to heed the safety rules described on page 178). Heat the oil to 360°F.

2. While the oil is heating, place your chou paste into a piping bag fitted with a medium star tip. Cut 18 squares of parchment paper, each 3 inches wide, and brush a little of the oil on one side of each piece. Pipe 2-inch circles of the chou paste onto the oiled sides of the parchment paper.

3. When the oil has reached 360°F, turn the heat down to the lowest setting to maintain heat during cooking. Pick up one of the strips of parchment paper and gently lower one end into the *friture*. The beignets will float and release themselves from the paper.

4. Discard the paper and fry the beignets in batches until golden brown, about 4 minutes, then carefully roll them over in the oil to cook the other side. When golden, lift the beignets out of the oil and drain on absorbent paper. Keep them warm.

5. When all of the beignets are cooked, dust them with powdered sugar and serve with warmed apricot sauce.

Profiteroles

Chou Buns with Pastry Cream and Chocolate Sauce

THIS SWEET TREAT showcases a good marriage of flavors that has stood the test of time. It's a classic French pastry that'll leave you hungry for more.

SERVES 6, MAKES 24 TO 30 PIECES

*1 recipe Pâte à Chou**

*1 cup Crème Pàtisserie**

2 tbsp Kirsch liqueur (optional)

½ cup heavy cream, whipped to stiff peaks

*1 recipe Sauce au Chocolat**

*For recipes and information about substitutions, see Fonds de Cuisine, page 175.

1. Use a piping bag with a ½-inch plain tip to pipe out balls (1 inch in diameter) of chou pastry onto a parchment paper-lined cookie sheet. Allow enough space between each ball (roughly their diameter) so they can rise during cooking without sticking to each other.

2. Cook the chou paste, following the directions on page 150.

3. Prepare the crème pàtisserie on page 189. When the pastry cream has cooled completely, beat it with a whisk until smooth, about 5 minutes; add the liqueur if desired. Gently fold in the stiffly whipped cream.

4. Make holes in the bases of the profiteroles. (I usually use the handle of a wooden spoon to do this.) Use a piping bag with a ¼-inch tip to pipe the enriched pastry cream into the profiteroles until they're full.

5. Arrange 4 to 5 profiteroles in each bowl or serving dish and pour the warmed chocolate sauce over them to serve.

Chaussons aux Pommes

Apple Turnovers

THE BEST APPLES to use for these chaussons are Cox's Orange Pippins. They combine great apple flavor with a wonderful balance of sweet and tart. These turnovers are delicious served warm at home, or take them on a picnic for a real countryside treat.

SERVES 8

½ recipe apple mixture prepared for Charlotte aux
   Pommes (page 162)

1 lb Puff Pastry*

All-purpose flour, as needed

½ cup sanding sugar (see note)

*For recipes and information about substitutions,
see Fonds de Cuisine, page 175.

1. Preheat the oven to 425°F.

2. Cook the apple mixture on the stove in a medium saucepan, covered, on medium heat until the apples break down to a pulp, about 10 minutes. Remove the lid and, stirring constantly, reduce the heat to low and cook the apples until they lose much of their liquid and become quite thick in consistency, 10 to 15 minutes. Be careful not to burn the mixture. Cool to room temperature and refrigerate until firm.

3. Divide the pastry in half. Dust a flat work surface very lightly with flour, as well as a light dusting on top of the pastry and your rolling pin. Use ½ of the pastry to create an 18-inch by 6-inch rectangle by rolling over the entire surface; use even pressure and roll up to but not over the edges.

4. Fold the rectangle in half lengthways, and then unfold it to show the center line. Spoon 2 tablespoons of the apple mixture at 4-inch intervals on the center line along the length of the pastry. Wet one of the long sides of the pastry with water and fold it over. Press the top edge of a cutter to crimp the pastry around the apple. Cut out turnovers using a fancy 4-inch cutter and making the cutouts about ½ inch outside the crimped line.

5. Repeat with the remaining pastry to make a total of 8 turnovers. Lightly brush the tops with a little water and immediately place them, damp side down, onto the sanding sugar.

6. Place the turnovers, sugar side up, onto a baking sheet sprayed with a light mist of water and bake for about 20 minutes, or until they're golden brown. Serve them warm or room temperature.

◇◇◇◇

NOTE:

Sanding sugar is a very coarse-grained granulated sugar. You may substitute granulated sugar if you have trouble finding it.

Clafouti aux Cerises

Cherry Clafouti

CLAFOUTI IS MADE with fresh fruit topped by a batter and baked. Cherries are the most popular fruit used for this dessert, but you may also try using peaches, apples, plums, or any other personal favorite.

SERVES 6

½ lb Pâte Brisée*

½ cup milk

½ cup heavy cream

1 vanilla bean

4 large eggs

1 cup plus 2 tbsp sugar, divided use

2 tsp Kirsch

1 tbsp all-purpose flour, sifted

1 lb ripe black cherries, pitted and left whole

*For recipes and information about substitutions, see Fonds de Cuisine, page 175.

1. Preheat the oven to 400°F.

2. Roll out the pâte brisée to ⅛ inch thick and line a 9-inch tart mold. Blind bake as directed on page 186. Remove the pastry from the oven and allow it to cool. Turn the oven down to 350°F.

3. Bring the milk, cream, and vanilla to a boil in a small saucepan; remove it immediately and cool it slightly. Beat the eggs, 1 cup of the sugar, and Kirsch together in a mixer until a thick foam is formed, about 10 to 15 minutes. Fold in the flour. Remove the vanilla bean from the milk and cream and add this mixture into the egg foam to form a batter.

4. Fill the tart shell with the cherries, and then pour the batter over the cherries. Bake the tart for 40 to 50 minutes, or until it has risen and is golden brown. Remove it from the oven and sprinkle the top with the remaining sugar. Allow the clafouti to cool slightly and serve while still nice and warm.

Tarte au Citron

Lemon Tart

THIS TART IS best when made the day before it will be served. It's delicious with crème fraîche!

MAKES ONE 9-INCH TART (ABOUT 8 TO 12 SERVINGS)

¾ lb Pâte Sucrée*

9 large eggs

2 large egg yolks

1¾ cups sugar

1¼ cups heavy cream

Zest and juice of 4 lemons

*For recipes and information about substitutions, see Fonds de Cuisine, page 175.

1. Preheat the oven to 375°F.

2. Roll out pâte sucrée to line a deep 9-inch quiche pan, ideally with a removable bottom. Blind bake as directed on page 186. Remove the pastry from the oven and allow it to cool. Turn the oven down to 300°F.

3. In a large bowl, beat the eggs, egg yolks,

and sugar together with a whisk until thoroughly mixed, about 3 minutes. In a separate medium size bowl, lightly beat the cream until a light froth forms on the surface, about 30 seconds. Combine the cream, egg mixture, lemon zest, and lemon juice and mix all together in the large bowl. The mix will curdle when you add the lemon; continue to whisk until the cur-

dle disappears. Put the custard in the refrigerator and chill.

4. Pour the custard through a fine-mesh strainer into the pastry crust. Bake the tart in the oven until the custard is set, 30 or 40 minutes.

6. Remove the tart from the oven and allow to cool before serving.

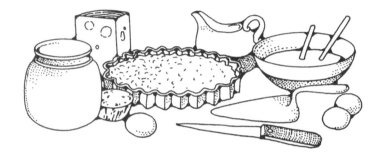

Tarte à la Rhubarbe

Rhubarb Tart

SERVES 6

½ lb puff pastry*

3½ cups sliced rhubarb (about 6 or 7 stalks)

¾ cup unsalted butter, melted

1 cup sugar

1-inch piece fresh ginger, peeled

1 cup crème fraîche*

*For recipes and information about substitutions, see Fonds de Cuisine, page 175.

1. Preheat the oven to 375°F.

2. Roll out the puff pastry to a circle 11 inches in diameter and about ⅛-inch thick and transfer to a baking sheet. Form a border in the pastry by roll-pleating the edge of the dough.

3. Arrange the rhubarb neatly on the pastry, in shingled layers in circles very close together. Brush them with melted butter and sprinkle them with the sugar.

4. Bake the tart for 45 minutes to 1 hour, or until the rhubarb is soft.

5. Finely grate the ginger and add it to the crème fraîche. Allow to steep in the refrigerator for at least 1 hour. Pass the cream through a cheesecloth to remove the ginger.

6. Allow the tart to cool for 30 minutes. Cut it into wedges and serve with the ginger cream.

Tarte aux Pommes

Apple Tart

COX'S ORANGE PIPPIN apples are the best choice for this treat. Their acidity, sweetness, and intense apple flavor make them ideal. If you can't find them in your area, try using Stayman, Winesap, Honeycrisp, Fuji, or Braeburn apples instead.

MAKES ONE 8-INCH TART (SERVES 6 TO 8)

¾ lb Pâte Sucrée*

4 lb pippin apples, peeled and cored

2 tbsp unsalted butter

2 tsp apricot jam

½ cup sugar

Zest and juice of 1 lemon

2-inch cinnamon stick

¼ cup unsalted butter, melted

¾ cup apricot glaze*

*For recipes and information about substitutions, see Fonds de Cuisine, page 175.

1. Preheat the oven to 350°F. Line a tart mold that is 8 inches in diameter and 1 inch deep with the pâte sucrée; prick the bottom with the point of your knife.

2. Roughly chop half of the prepared apples. Melt 2 tablespoons of the butter and 2 teaspoons of the apricot jam in a medium saucepan over medium heat. Add the chopped apples, ½ cup of sugar, lemon juice and zest, and the cinnamon stick. Cover with a lid and cook on medium heat until the apples begin to break up, 10 to 15 minutes.

3. Drain off the juice from these apples into a small saucepan and reduce this liquid over medium heat by half, about 10 minutes. Pour the reduced juice back into the pan with the cooked apples and stir. Remove the cinnamon stick. Put the apple mixture to one side and let it cool.

4. Pour the cooled apple filling into the pastry-lined tart mold. Slice the remaining apples thinly, about ⅛ inch thick. Fan the slices in ever-decreasing circles until the cooked apple mix is completely covered. Brush the top of the tart with melted butter.

5. Bake the tart in the oven for 45 minutes, until the pastry is golden and the apple slices have brown edges. Remove the tart from the oven and heat the apricot glaze until it barely reaches a simmer. Brush the top of the tart with the glaze, allow it to cool to room temperature, and serve.

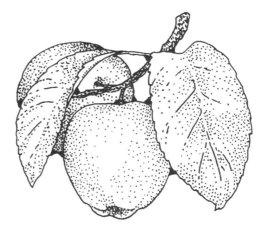

Tarte Tatin

Caramelized Apple Tart

WE'VE TAKEN A few liberties with the classic tarte tatin to create an individual dessert. The apple you choose should be good for baking, which means it will become very tender but still keep its shape.

MAKES 4 INDIVIDUAL SERVINGS

CARAMEL

1 cup sugar

6 tbsp water

1 tbsp corn syrup

2 large Stayman, Honeycrisp, or Braeburn apples, peeled and cored (8 oz each)

Juice of 1 lemon

¼ cup unsalted butter

1 sheet Puff Pastry*

4 mint sprigs

*For recipes and information about substitutions, see Fonds de Cuisine, page 175.

1. Preheat the oven to 375°F. Combine the sugar and water in a medium saucepan on medium heat and bring to a boil. Stir to dissolve all the sugar, then add the corn syrup. Turn the heat up to high. Use a pastry brush dipped in clean water to wash away the sugar deposits on the inside of the pan until the sugar stops splashing the sides. When the mix starts to caramelize and becomes a golden brown, take the caramel off the heat and immediately pour into four 8-ounce ramekin molds, to a depth of ³⁄₁₆ inch each.

2. Slice the apples in half vertically. Lay the dome side down into the molds. Pour 1 teaspoon of lemon juice over each apple in the molds. Add 1 tablespoon of butter in the dip of each apple where the core used to be. *(recipe continues on next page)*

3. Roll out the puff pastry to ⅛ inch thick; allow it to rest for 30 minutes. Cut four 4½-inch circles with a fluted pastry wheel and place them on top of the apples.

4. Bake the apples in the oven for approximately 45 minutes, or until the pastry is golden brown. To check if the apples are done, use a paring knife to lift the puff pastry slightly. The apples are done when they look translucent; there should be no resistance in the apple.

5. Cool the tarts slightly for about 5 minutes; turn the ramekins over onto a tray. Let the pastries sit for about 5 more minutes and take the molds off. Place a mint *plûche* (a bit of the sprig) at the top of the apple and serve with ice cream.

◇◇◇◇

NOTE:

Be careful of steam burns when lifting up the pastry to check the apple underneath. *Do not* use your fingers to do this—you'll never be quicker than the steam escaping from the ramekins, and the resulting burn would undoubtedly mar your enjoyment of the dessert.

Tarte au Pêche et Fromage de Chèvre

Peach and Goat Cheese Tarts

MAKES ONE 9-INCH TART (SERVES 8)

*½ lb Pâte Sucrée**

4 oz goat cheese

3 large egg yolks

½ cup sugar

1 tsp vanilla extract (preferably Bourbon)

Zest of ¼ lemon

½ tsp lemon juice

1½ cups half-and-half

2 peaches

¼ cup sugar for glazing

*For recipes and information about substitutions, see Fonds de Cuisine, page 175.

1.Preheat the oven to 375°F. Roll out the pâte sucrée to line a 9-inch tart. Blind bake as directed on page 186. Remove the pastry from the oven and allow it to cool. Turn the oven down to 350°F.

2. To prepare the custard, mix the cheese, egg yolks, sugar, vanilla, zest, and lemon juice together in a bowl until it's smooth.

3. Heat the half-and-half in a medium saucepan over medium heat until it's scalded, 5 to 10 minutes, and then cool for 5 minutes. Pour the warm half-and-half into the cheese mixture and stir it thoroughly.

4. Peel the peaches, cut them in half, and remove the stones. Cut the halves into slices—you should get 8 slices from each half. Lay the slices abstractly into the baked pastry, which is still in its tart mold. Place the peach-filled tart onto a cookie sheet and pour the cheese custard into the tart until it's full. Carefully place the tray into the oven and bake the tart for about 30 minutes, or until the custard is set.

5. Remove the tart from the oven, cool it to room temperature, and sprinkle it with the sugar. Glaze the sugar with a blow torch or very hot broiler. Serve immediately, or allow it to cool slightly before serving.

Charlotte aux Pommes

Apple Charlotte

THIS DESSERT IS traditionally served with apricot sauce, but goes equally well with vanilla sauce or vanilla ice cream. It's useful to use ovenproof, clear glass ramekins for this, because you can see when the charlotte has turned golden.

SERVES 6 TO 8

3 lb peeled pippin apples, cored and chopped

1½ cup unsalted butter, melted, divided use

6 tbsp apricot glaze* or jam

1 cinnamon stick

½ cup sugar

Juice and zest of 1 lemon

1 brioche loaf, or fine-grained sliced white bread

1 cup unsalted butter, melted

*For recipes and information about substitutions, see Fonds de Cuisine, page 175.

1. Preheat the oven to 375°F.

2. Stew the apples on low heat in a tightly covered medium pot, with ½ cup of the melted butter, apricot glaze or jam, cinnamon stick, sugar, lemon juice, and zest until they're slightly softened, 10 to 15 minutes. Strain the juice into another pan and reduce it by two-thirds, 5 to 10 minutes. Return the juice to the pan with the apples and let it cool.

3. Cut the brioche lengthways into ¼-inch-thick slices. Cut out 12 disks of brioche to fit into the bases and tops of your 6-ounce molds and cut strips to line the walls; these strips should not exceed the top edges of the molds.

4. Dip one side of each brioche piece into the remaining melted butter, and then use the pieces to line the molds. Make sure the buttered surfaces are facing out in the molds and that the strips are slightly overlapping. This will help develop a golden crust. You should have 6 round disks left over to cover each filled mold.

5. Fill the brioche-lined molds with apple mixture until it's slightly above the top of the mold. Cover each top with a disk of buttered brioche, making sure that the butter is facing out, and bake them in the oven for 30 to 40 minutes, or until golden brown.

6. Remove the charlottes from the oven and cool them for 5 minutes before turning them out onto plates or a serving platter.

Merveilles

Deep-Fried Dough Pastries

THESE TRADITIONAL PASTRIES from Southern France are prepared in a variety of shapes (different shapes are popular in the different towns of the region). The dough is cut into pieces with a knife or different-shaped cookie cutters, which are then deep-fried and dusted with powdered sugar. Enjoy them hot or cold—they'll stay fresh for several days in a sealed container.

SERVES 6

4 cups all-purpose flour, plus more for dusting

½ cup unsalted butter, soft

6 large eggs

Salt as needed

2 tsp vanilla extract

2 tsp baking powder

3 tsp rose water

2 tbsp Armagnac

Zest of ½ lemon

1 qt oil for frying

Powdered sugar for dusting

1. Mix the first 9 ingredients together in a mixing bowl fitted with a dough hook attachment. Mix on the lowest speed for 2 minutes, until you have soft, pliable dough. Refrigerate the dough, covered, for 1 hour.

2. On a lightly floured board, roll out the dough as thinly as possible. Use a knife or cutters to cut the dough into any shape you want.

3. Follow the deep-frying precautions listed on page 178 when doing the next few steps. Heat the oil to 360°F and begin frying the dough pieces. Turn them over occasionally to brown evenly. When they're crisp and puffy, after about 6 minutes, remove them from the oil and drain them on absorbent paper or a napkin.

4. Keep the pastries warm while you fry the remainder of the dough. Try not to eat too many in the meantime.

5. Dust the finished pastries with powdered sugar and enjoy the rest!

Poires Poché au Roquefort

Poached Pears with Roquefort

THERE IS NOTHING timid about this dessert! Pears are a favored fruit in France. Here, gently poached to a brilliant claret in a bold red wine and served in a sauce finished with ruby port and red currant jelly, pears are combined with creamy, salty, and pungent Roquefort cheese for a classic bistro dessert.

MAKES 6 SERVINGS

1¼ cups full-bodied red wine

½ cup sugar

10 tbsp port

4 tbsp red-currant jelly

1¼ cups water

1 cinnamon stick

1 strip lemon zest

6 pears, William, Doyonne de Comice, Bartlett, or Bosc

1 ¼ cups Roquefort cheese

1. Boil the first 7 ingredients in a saucepan on medium heat until the sugar is dissolved, about 5 minutes. Be certain to use a pan large enough to accommodate the pears standing up when you're ready to add them.

2. Peel the pears but leave the stems on. Cut a thin slice from the base of each pear to facilitate standing. Add the pears to the wine. Place them close enough together in the pan to ensure the wine comes up high enough to poach them properly.

3. Simmer the pears for 20 to 30 minutes, or until they're just soft on the outside. Remove them with a slotted spoon and allow them to cool to room temperature.

4. Reduce the cooking liquid *(cuisson)* over medium heat until it's syrupy. Be careful not to over-reduce because you may caramelize the sugars and have the wrong flavor.

5. Crumble the Roquefort and keep it in the refrigerator.

6. Cut the pears in half lengthways but leave the stalk in place on one side. Remove the core from each half. Thinly slice the pear halves and shingle them on the plate, leaning them against one another. Coat the slices with the reduced sauce and sprinkle them with the Roquefort.

◇◇◇◇

NOTE:

Be careful of testing your pear with the point of a knife because what may be barely visible now will become a gaping wound later, thus affecting your final presentation.

Crème Brûlée

Sugar-Glazed Custard

MANY PEOPLE FEEL the need to place various fruits on the surface of the crème brûlées as a garnish. Very pretty, but the liquid/juices coming from these fruits will dissolve your crisp layer, thus denying the diner the true crème brûlée experience.

MAKES 6 INDIVIDUAL SERVINGS

7 tbsp sugar

6 large egg yolks

1 vanilla bean

¼ cup milk

2 cups heavy cream

½ cup sugar, for brûléeing the tops

1. Preheat the oven to 325°F. Whisk the sugar and egg yolks together in a large bowl until thoroughly mixed, about 2 minutes.

2. Split the vanilla bean and scrape out the seeds. Add the seeds and bean to the milk and cream and heat in a medium saucepan over medium heat until it's scalded, about 10 minutes. Remove the mix from the heat and allow it to cool for 10 minutes. Pour this hot mixture onto the beaten eggs and sugar and mix the custard thoroughly. Pass this custard through a fine-mesh strainer sieve (chinois).

3. Divide the custard among six 4-ounce ramekin molds. Place the filled molds into a hot water bath (bain-marie), and cook them in the oven for 30 to 40 minutes, or until just set. They should jiggle slightly when shaken.

4. Cool the custards to room temperature and then chill, uncovered, in the refrigerator.

5. When the custards are completely cooled, about 2 hours, sprinkle an even layer (about 1/16 inch) of the sugar over each one. Glaze them (*brûlée*) either under the broiler or with a blowtorch; the sugar will melt and turn a light golden color. Once it's properly caramelized, it will form a hard crust that cracks when you tap it with a spoon.

6. Serve the crème brûlées immediately in the ramekins.

◇◇◇◇◇◇◇

CHEF'S TIP:

Successful glazing (bruléeing) depends greatly upon an even layer of the right amount of sugar, a dry surface on the custard and, when using a blowtorch, even heating.

The beauty of this dish lies in its simplicity. The strength is its contrasting textures between a thin, crisp layer of sugar covering sublime creaminess.

CRÈME CARAMEL

Caramelized Custard

⸺⸺

MAKES 6 INDIVIDUAL SERVINGS

CARAMEL

1 cup sugar, plus as needed to coat molds

1 cup cold water, divided use

Softened butter as needed for molds

CUSTARD

2⅓ cups milk

1 vanilla bean

3 large eggs

3 tbsp sugar

1. Preheat the oven to 300°F. To make the caramel, combine the sugar and ¾ cup water in a medium saucepan over medium heat. Stir gently until the sugar is completely dissolved. Bring to a boil over high heat. When the mix starts to caramelize and becomes a golden brown, immediately take the caramel off the heat and add ¼ cup cold water. (The water will spatter and foam up, so keep your hands and arms out of harm's way. Adding cold water to the hot caramel now stops the sugar from overcooking or turning too bitter.) Return the pan to the heat and bring the caramel back to a boil. When the second boil is reached, take the pan from the heat and pour a ⅛-inch layer into the bottom of six 6-ounce molds.

As soon as the molds are cool enough to handle, brush the sides of the molds with softened butter and sprinkle with a little additional sugar.

2. To prepare the crème, heat the milk with the vanilla bean in a medium saucepan on medium heat until it's scalded, about 8 minutes. Cool for 5 minutes, and then remove the bean. (Save this vanilla bean to make vanilla sugar or to use in another dish.) Beat together the eggs and sugar in a medium bowl until they're just combined, then add the scalded milk, whisking gently as you add the milk so the eggs don't scramble.

3. Strain the custard through a fine-mesh sieve into the molds while the custard is still warm (between 110 and 120°F). Set the molds in a deep baking dish and place the baking dish on your oven rack. Add enough boiling water to rise about half way up the sides of the mold. Place a cookie sheet or aluminum foil over the top of the baking dish to prevent a skin from forming.

4. Cook the custards in the water bath (bain-marie) until they're just set, 35 to 40 minutes, or until the custards jiggle slightly in the middle. Remove them from the bain-marie and cool for 2 to 3 hours. These are best when served cold.

5. To serve, turn the custards out onto plates; there's no need to run a knife around them to release them from the molds.

Mousse au Chocolat

Chocolate Mousse

**SERVES 10 IN 4-OUNCE RAMEKINS OR
5 TO 6 IN 5-OUNCE GLASSES**

5 large egg yolks

2 shots hot espresso coffee

2 tbsp Vanilla Sugar*

8 oz dark chocolate, melted

MERINGUE

4 large egg whites

¼ cup sugar

¾ cup heavy cream, whipped to soft peaks

Whipped cream for garnish

*For recipes and information about substitutions,
see Fonds de Cuisine, page 175.

1. Beat the yolks with the espresso and vanilla sugar until a mousse-like foam is achieved, 10 to 15 minutes. Stir in the melted chocolate. Set aside while preparing the meringue.

2. In a clean bowl, whip the egg whites to a thick foam (you can do this with a whisk or in a mixing machine) and add the sugar gradually while still beating. Continue to whip after all the sugar is added until you have a soft, glossy meringue, about 5 minutes. Fold the meringue into the chocolate mixture in two or three additions, just until it is evenly blended. (The meringue will deflate a little as you work, but adding it in parts helps keep it as light as possible.) Fold in the ¾ cup of whipped cream.

3. Immediately spoon or pipe the mousse mixture into molds (stemmed glasses such as brandy snifters or wine glasses, custard cups, or soufflé dishes are all good options). Chill the mousse at least 3 hours before serving. Spoon or pipe a dollop or rosette of the whipped cream on top of each mousse.

Petits Pots de Crème au Chocolat

Little Pots of Chocolate Cream

SERVES 6

½ cup sugar

¾ cup milk

¾ cup heavy cream

½ vanilla bean

1 shot of espresso

2 oz dark chocolate

1 large egg, lightly beaten

3 large egg yolks, lightly beaten

¼ cup heavy cream, whipped to stiff peak,
    for garnish

1. Preheat the oven to 350°F. Place the sugar in a thick-bottomed pan over low heat and stir until it's melted. Once it's melted, slowly swirl the pan over the heat to keep the temperature even. Continue swirling until the sugar turns golden, 5 to 10 minutes. Add the milk, cream, and vanilla bean. Simmer this mix gently for 5 minutes, or until the caramel has dissolved into the milk and cream.

2. Add the espresso and chocolate and whisk it over medium heat until it's smooth, about 2 minutes. Allow it to cool for 5 minutes.

3. Pour this mix into the beaten egg and egg yolks, mix it thoroughly, and pass it through a fine-mesh strainer. Pour the mixture into 4- or 5-ounce ramekins or petits pots molds.

4. Bake the chocolate in a water bath (bain-marie) in the oven until it's set—the center should jiggle slightly. This should take 20 to 30 minutes. Remove the chocolate from the water bath and allow it to cool completely.

5. Serve this delicious dessert decorated with whipped cream.

GLACE AUX PRUNEAUX À L'ARMAGNAC

Prune and Armagnac Ice Cream

———⎯⎯⎯⎯———

THIS CLASSIC ICE CREAM from the southwest of France celebrates an ingredient with a dubious reputation in this country. This has to be, in my humble opinion, one of the most enjoyable ways to enjoy prunes (dried plums). True Agen prunes are the finest in the world, and have been granted AOC status. From the southwest of France, not far from Gascony. true Agen prunes have an unmatched depth of flavor, so if you can find them, do try them in this recipe. Pairing this much-maligned fruit with its regional neighbor, Armagnac, is sheer genius. Oh, those cunning French!

SERVES 6

1 cup prunes (preferably Agen prunes)

⅔ cup Armagnac

1 recipe Vanilla Ice Cream (page 172)

1. Pit the prunes and cut them into raisin-size pieces. Pour the Armagnac over them and allow them to steep in the refrigerator for 24 hours.

2. Add the prunes to your ice cream mix when it's almost finished churning; add some of the Armagnac in which the prunes steeped, to taste.

Crème Glacée à la Vanille

Vanilla Ice Cream

MAKES 3 PINTS

2 cups milk

2 cups heavy cream

2 vanilla beans, split lengthwise

¾ cup sugar, divided use

12 large egg yolks

1. Cook the milk, cream, and vanilla beans in a medium saucepan on the stove over medium heat. Add half of the sugar and stir until you can't feel any more crystals on the bottom of the pan. Bring the mix to a boil but do not stir. The layer of sugar will prevent the milk from burning.

2. Beat the egg yolks along with the remaining sugar in a bowl until thick foam has formed, about 5 to 10 minutes. Once the milk and cream have come to the boil, turn off the heat and place the bowl containing the eggs over the hot milk and cream. Continue to whip the eggs over the heat until you raise their temperature to 110°F, about another 5 minutes. Remove them from the heat.

3. Bring the milk and cream back to a boil. When the milk and cream start to look like they'll boil over, pour the mix all at once into the eggs while whisking thoroughly. When done, the mix should be able to coat the back of a spoon and leave a clear channel when you draw a finger through it.

4. Pour this mixture through a fine-mesh strainer into a container set over ice. Stir it occasionally to expedite cooling. Once the mixture has cooled to room temperature, place it in your refrigerator to chill overnight.

5. Churn in an ice cream machine according to the manufacturer's instructions.

◇◇◇◇◇◇◇◇◇

CHEF'S NOTE:

This method of cooking the base for an ice cream is used in the industry to save time. Have a bowl of ice and water ready in order to cool the mixture immediately after cooking. This prevents it from curdling. If your ice cream does curdle, an easy way to bring it back is to use an immersion blender for 3 to 5 seconds, which will reemulsify the custard.

Fonds de Cuisine

UNDERSTANDING THE FRENCH culinary term *mise en place,* or "putting in place," is essential for the professional chef and home cook alike. At its most basic level, it refers to assembling all ingredients, tools, and pans required to prepare a meal. But mise en place is also a state of mind. In a busy restaurant kitchen, careful planning allows a chef to keep many tasks in mind simultaneously, arranging steps and assigning priorities as needed. In your own kitchen, the same methodical approach will make the process of cooking less hectic and more enjoyable.

Keep in mind that convenience products can shave valuable time from meal preparation. Canned broth and stocks or frozen doughs can be real timesavers, as are canned beans. Sample different brands until you find ones that best suit your taste.

DONENESS OF MEATS AND POULTRY

Temperature is the most accurate method for judging the doneness of meat. Use an instant-read thermometer or a meat thermometer that stays in the meat while it cooks. Except for rare beef and lamb, the temperatures in the chart on page 176 conform to the USDA's recommendations, but you may choose to adjust them to suit your taste.

While temperature is a key indicator of doneness, experienced cooks rely on all their senses to evaluate meats as they cook and to judge doneness, as well as using thermometers. The cooking time quoted in a recipe can help you plan when to start cooking but by itself is not an accurate way to determine a meat's doneness. Touching meat to judge its firmness offers a helpful guideline that restaurant chefs use frequently to gauge the progression of cooking. With the tip of one finger, press the meat at the center of the cut to judge its resistance. The less done a piece of meat is, the softer and more yielding it will feel. Braised or simmered meats are often considered done when they are fork tender; that is, when a fork slides easily into and out of the cooked meat. Assess how the meat tastes once it is finished cooking and make notes to help you remember for the next time.

Temperature is the best way to determine doneness in poultry as well as meat. To test the temperature, insert an instant-read meat thermometer in the thickest part of the flesh. Keep the tip of the thermometer away from the bird's bones, which can skew the reading. In bigger birds, residual heat continues to cook the meat after it is removed from the oven. The internal temperature of a whole turkey or goose may rise another 10°F on average as it rests, so the bird may be removed from the oven before the final temperature is reached. Other, less accurate tests of doneness in poultry are checking that legs move easily in their sockets; checking that juices run clear when a thigh is pierced; checking that breast meat is firm and opaque throughout; and checking that the meat of legs, thighs, and wings releases easily from the bone.

TESTING FISH AND SHELLFISH FOR DONENESS

In general, cook seafood until it registers 145°F on an instant-read thermometer, or until the flesh is opaque. Well-cooked fish will separate easily into

DONENESS TEMPERATURES AND TESTS

DEGREE OF DONENESS	FINAL RESTING TEMP.	DESCRIPTION
Beef, Veal, and Lamb:		
Rare	135°F	Interior is red and shiny.
Medium Rare	145°F	Rosy pink interior, juicy.
Medium	160°F	Pink only at center, pale pink juices.
Well done	170°F	Evenly brown throughout, no traces of red or pink, moist but no juices.
Pork:		
Medium	160°F	Opaque throughout, slight give, juices with faint blush.
Well done	170°F	Slight give, juices clear.
Poultry:		
Whole birds	180°F	Legs move easily in sockets and when pierced in the thigh, juices run clear. Juices in an unstuffed bird's cavity no longer have a red or pink hue.
Breasts	170°F	Meat becomes opaque and firm throughout.
Legs, thighs, and wings	180°F	Meat easily releases from the bone.
Stuffing	165°F	For stuffing cooked separately or inside a whole bird.
Ground poultry	165°F	Even color throughout, opaque, no hint of pink.

flakes when prodded with a fork but should still be moist. Meaty fish such as salmon, tuna, or swordfish is sometimes cooked to medium-rare, or still translucent in the center. As with red meat, seafood will become more firm and less springy as it cooks. Press fish gently with a finger to help determine doneness, as well as checking the internal temperature. The shells of shrimp, lobster, and crab will turn vivid pink or bright red and their flesh will become opaque when cooked through. Scallops will turn milky white and feel firm to the touch. The shells of bivalves such as clams, mussels, and oysters will open once properly cooked. Discard any shellfish whose shells remain closed after cooking, because they were likely dead before cooking.

Resting roasts before carving

As foods roast, their juices become concentrated at the center. Letting whole poultry and other roasts rest before serving gives the juices time to redistribute evenly throughout the bird and firms the meat for better slicing. Resting also allows the temperature of the meat to equalize, thus improving its texture, aroma, and flavor. After you remove a roast from the oven, leave it in a warm place. Allow a resting time of 5 minutes for small roasts and up to 30 minutes for a large roast.

Monté au Beurre

Monté au beurre is a finishing technique that adds a touch of additional richness and finish to sauces. To be successful, the sauce must already be somewhat thickened, a state known in French as *nappé*. It means that the sauce is thick enough to lightly coat the back of a spoon. To monté au beurre, have cubes or slices of chilled butter ready. The sauce should be over very low heat, not boiling rapidly. Add one or two pieces of butter at a time to the sauce and either swirl the pan over the burner until the butter is worked into the sauce or whisk it gently. The sauce's texture will lighten somewhat, and it will have a satiny sheen if the butter is properly blended in.

Toasted Flour

Toasted flour is easy to prepare and stores well. You can use it to thicken sauces, soups, stews, and braises. Preheat the oven to 350°F and spread a thin layer of all-purpose flour on a baking sheet or pan. Toast the flour in the oven, stirring it occasionally so it browns evenly. When the flour is a golden brown, remove it from the oven and pour it into a cool bowl. After the flour cools down, sift it to break up any clumps. Transfer to a storage container. The flour will keep almost indefinitely in a cool, dry area.

Making Clarified Butter

Clarified butter, unlike whole butter, can be used for sautéing since it can reach higher temperatures without smoking or burning. While it can't reach temperatures as high as cooking oils, it has the advantage of giving foods as rich, buttery flavor.

To make clarified butter, heat whole butter in a heavy saucepan over very low heat until foam rises to the surface and the milk solids drop to the bottom. As the remaining butterfat becomes clear, skim the surface to remove all traces of the foam. Pour or ladle off the butterfat into another container, taking care to leave behind all of the water and milk solids at the bottom of the pan.

One pound of whole butter yields approximately twelve ounces of clarified butter. Clarified butter can be stored in the refrigerator for up to 2 weeks.

MAKING LARDONS

Lardons can only be made from slab bacon. They are more substantial than minced bacon bits, and deserve a little care in preparation if they are to be enjoyed at their best. Apart from adding a rich flavor, lardons are also cooked in the early stages of preparing a number of dishes to release their flavorful fat, a procedure known as rendering.

To cut lardons, first cut the rind away from the piece of slab bacon. (You can add this piece to stock or soups as they simmer to get every bit of flavor out of your bacon.) Slice the bacon into ¼ inch thick slices. Turn these slices 90 degrees and cut at right angles, so that each piece contains layers of fat and lean meat. Place them in a large heavy-bottomed pan or casserole with a bit of olive oil. Set the pan over on medium or low heat and cook gently, stirring to let the lardons brown and crisp evenly. This may take up to 5 minutes. Keep the heat gentle if you want to release the fat into the pan. When the lardons are crisp and golden, lift them out of the pan with a slotted spoon. Drain them briefly on paper towels.

PRECAUTIONS FOR DEEP FRYING FOODS

Always take these precautions when frying foods in an open pan on the stove *(friture):*

1. Never fill the pan more than one-third full with the oil.

2. Make sure you do not exceed 360°F.

2. Wet foods must be dried before plunging them into the oil.

4. Do not overload the friture.

Ignoring any of these safety tips may result in a fire!

CRÈME FRAÎCHE

Many stores carry crème fraîche, but you can make your own. It takes just a little effort to produce this thick, slightly tangy crème. The French have long known that crème fraîche is a better choice than either sour cream or yogurt to finish hot dishes like soups and sauces because it doesn't "break" when it is heated.

First, sterilize an empty 1-pint capacity jar as follows: Put the jar on a rack or a folded cloth in a deep pot. Drop in the lid at the same time. Add enough hot water to fill and completely cover the jar. Bring the water to a boil and continue boiling for 10 minutes. Use tongs to carefully lift the jar and lid out of the water and empty them. Set them on a clean cloth.

Next, pour in 1½ cups heavy cream and ¼ cup cultured buttermilk. Cover the jar, shake the contents to blend them, and let the mixture sit at room temperature for at least 12 hours, or until it is thickened. The crème is ready to use now, or you can store it in the refrigerator for up to 1 week.

WHIPPING CREAM

Heavy cream may be whipped to soft or medium peaks for use in sweet and savory applications.

Chilling the cream as well as the bowl and whisk or beaters helps produce a more stable foam that holds volume when folded into other ingredients.

Use a balloon whisk or electric mixer to whip

cream. Begin whipping the cream at a moderate speed. Once the cream begins to thicken, increase the speed and continue to whip until the cream reaches the desired thickness. Cream may be whipped to soft peaks or medium peaks.

Avoid overbeating the cream, as it will lose much of its flexibility as well as its sheen and velvety texture. Cream will eventually turn to butter if the whipping continues.

For best results, sugar and other flavorings should be added after the cream is whipped to soft peaks. Cream that has been sweetened with confectioners' sugar and flavored with vanilla is called *chantilly cream*.

BAIN MARIE

A bain marie is a hot water bath, used either in the oven or on the stovetop to cook foods very gently and evenly. A double boiler is an example of a saucepan with a second pan or bowl that nests on top. You can make a bain marie by finding two pots that can "nest." The large pot should be able to hold an inch or two of water. The smaller pot (or even a mixing bowl) is then set in the hot water.

To make a bain marie for foods cooked in the oven, like custards, set the baking pan or mold in a large, deep baking or roasting pan. Place in the oven, and then add enough boiling water to the outer pan to come part way up the sides of the molds. You may wish to cover the pan as the food cooks by putting a baking sheet over the top of the pan or tenting it loosely with aluminum foil or parchment paper.

Do not let the water boil; adjust the heat to maintain a slow simmer.

BOUQUET GARNI AND SACHET D'ÉPICES

Bouquet garni and sachet d'épices are two basic aromatic preparations called for over and over again. These combinations of aromatic vegetables, herbs, and spices are meant to enhance and support the flavors of a dish infusing them with flavor, in the same way that a teabag is used to make a cup of tea. Certain basic techniques and ingredient proportions should be observed as outlined in the following methods for both bouquets garni and sachets d'épices.

A bouquet garni is made up of fresh herbs and vegetables tied into a bundle. If a leek is used to wrap the other bouquet garni ingredients, it must be thoroughly rinsed first to remove the dirt. Enclose the herbs in the leek leaves or celery. Cut a piece of string long enough to leave a tail to tie the bouquet to the pot handle. This makes it easy to pull out the bouquet when it is time to remove it.

A sachet contains such ingredients as peppercorns, other spices, or herbs tied up in a cheesecloth bag.

The standard recipes for bouquet garni and sachet d'épices can be modified a little (add some carrot or a garlic clove) or a lot (use cardamom, ginger, ground turmeric, and cinnamon) to produce different effects. Some of our recipes indicate a special addition.

A STANDARD BOUQUET GARNI INCLUDES:

1 sprig of thyme

3 or 4 parsley stems

1 bay leaf

2 or 3 leek leaves and/or 1 celery stalk cut crosswise in half

3 or 4 parsley stems

1 sprig of thyme or 1 teaspoon dried thyme

1 bay leaf

1 tsp cracked peppercorns.

WHITE WINE VINAIGRETTE

MAKES 2 CUPS

½ cup white wine vinegar

1 tsp Dijon-style mustard

Salt and pepper as needed

¾ cup extra-virgin olive oil

¾ cup corn or safflower oil

2 to 3 tbsp minced herbs, optional

Whisk together the vinegar, mustard, about ½ teaspoon salt, and a pinch of black pepper. Gradually whisk in the oils until they are all incorporated and the vinaigrette is smooth and lightly thickened (as the vinaigrette sits, it will start to separate). Season with minced herbs, if using, and additional salt and pepper, if needed.

SHERRY VINAIGRETTE

MAKES 1 CUP

¼ cup sherry vinegar

1 tbsp minced shallots

1 tbsp chopped parsley

1 tsp chopped thyme

1 tbsp chopped parsley

1 tsp honey (optional)

¾ cup olive oil

In a medium bowl, combine all the ingredients except the olive oil. Gradually whisk in the olive oil until the dressing is lightly thickened. Taste and adjust the seasoning.

DUXELLES

MAKES ABOUT 1 CUP

2 tbsp clarified butter (page 177)

½ cup minced onions

1 tbsp minced shallot

2 cups minced mushrooms

2 tbsp dry white wine

Salt and pepper as needed

½ tsp minced tarragon (optional)

2 tsp minced chives (optional)

Heat the butter in a sauté pan over medium high heat. Add the onions and shallot and cook, stirring frequently, until the onions are tender and translucent, about 4 minutes. Add the mushrooms and cook, stirring, until the moisture released by the mushrooms has cooked away, about 10 minutes. Add the wine and cook until the wine has reduced. Season with salt and pepper. Stir in the tarragon and chives, if using. (Duxelles can be made in advance and stored in the refrigerator for up to 1 week.)

To use as a stuffing, add enough fresh white bread crumbs to lightly bind the duxelles together.

CROUTONS

Store-bought croutons are available, and some are evenly fresh prepared right in the store. But you can certainly make your own following the instructions here. Once prepared, you can store croutons in an air-tight container at room temperature for up to 4 days. Cut your croutons to the size and shape you prefer. Some classic dishes call for heart-shaped croutons. Large croutons are good to serve as the bed for a steak or grilled food or as a major garnish for a soup. Smaller croutons cut into cubes are great for garnishing salads, omelettes, and soups.

Choose a bread with a firm, even grain. Cut the crusts away from the bread and then cut the croutons into the shape you prefer. Add enough clarified butter to a sauté pan to come to a depth of about ¼ inch. Add the croutons in batches and cook, turning as necessary, until they are an even, golden brown. Let the croutons drain briefly on absorbent toweling.

Croutons can be seasoned before or after you cook them in the butter with ingredients such as garlic, grated cheese, salt and pepper, or fresh or dried herbs.

SAUCE RAIFORT

Horseradish Sauce

MAKES 1 CUP

¾ cup crème fraîche (page 178) or sour cream

3 tbsp grated horseradish, drained

1 tbsp minced shallot

2 tsp lemon juice, or as needed

½ tsp salt

¼ tsp pepper

Combine all of the ingredients in a bowl and stir until smooth. Refrigerate until needed. This sauce can be stored in the refrigerator for up to 2 days.

STOCKS AND SAUCES

Purchased stock (or broth) is a fine substitution in almost any recipe, as long as you take the time to seek out a brand with a flavor and texture you like. Some brands may be a little fattier, others may be saltier than you like. Take the time to taste the stock or broth on its own to be sure it has the taste you want.

You can use the stock recipes below to make a wide range of stocks, from brown stocks to game stocks to vegetable stocks. See the variation notes following the basic recipes for some options.

For the clearest stock, be sure to skim the liquid frequently as it comes to a simmer and as often as necessary thereafter. Never let it reach a boil; this will make the stock cloudy. In describing the proper state of a broth as it simmers, the French use the verb *fremir*—to tremble. This means that there should be movement on the surface, but only a few lazy bubbles should be seen breaking the surface.

CHICKEN STOCK

MAKES ABOUT 2 QUARTS

4 lb chicken pieces or meaty bones, such as backs and necks

3 qt cold water

1 large onion, diced (about 1¼ cups)

1 carrot, diced (about ⅓ cup)

1 celery stalk, diced (about ½ cup)

1 bouquet garni (page 179)

1. Place the chicken and water in a large pot (the water should cover the chicken by at least two inches; add more if necessary). Bring the water slowly to a boil over medium heat.

2. As the water comes to a boil, skim away any foam that rises to the surface. Adjust the heat once a boil is reached so that a slow, lazy simmer is established. Cover partially and simmer for 2 hours, skimming as often as necessary.

3. Add all of the remaining ingredients. Continue to simmer, skimming the surface as necessary, until the stock is fully flavored, about 1 hour.

4. Strain the stock through a colander or sieve into a large metal container. Discard the solids. If you are using the stock right away, skim off any fat on the surface. If you are not using the stock right away, store in the refrigerator for up to 5 days, or in the freezer for up to 3 months.

DUCK STOCK: Replace the chicken pieces or bones with duck bones. Prepare as directed.

BEEF STOCK

MAKES ABOUT 2 QUARTS

4 lb beef (chuck, ribs, shank, or neck)

3 qt water

1½ medium onions, coarsely chopped (about 2 cups)

1 leek, white and light green part, coarsely chopped (about 1¼ cups)

1 carrot, coarsely chopped (about ⅓ cup)

1 celery stalk, coarsely chopped (about ½ cup)

¼ cup celery leaves

3 to 4 parsley stems

3 to 4 black peppercorns

1 bay leaf

2 tsp salt, or to taste

1 sprig fresh thyme or ½ tsp dried thyme

1. Preheat the oven to 400°F.

2. Put the beef in a roasting pan and place in the oven. Roast the beef until deep brown, about 45 minutes to 1 hour. Transfer the beef to a soup pot. Pour 1 cup of the water into the hot roasting pan and scrape the bottom to loosen any drippings; pour over the beef. Add the remaining water (there should be enough to cover the beef by 2 inches; add more water if necessary) and bring to a simmer. Cover partially and simmer gently for 2 hours. Frequently skim away any scum that rises to the surface.

3. Add the remaining ingredients. Continue to simmer gently until the stock has developed a full, rich flavor, about 2 hours. Remove the meat and reserve for another use.

4. Strain the stock through a fine sieve or cheesecloth-lined colander into a large metal container. Discard the solids.

5. If you are using the stock right away, skim off any fat on the surface. If you are not using the stock right away, cool it quickly by placing the container in a sink filled with ice cold water. Stir the stock as it cools, and then transfer it to storage containers. Store in the refrigerator for up to 5 days, or in the freezer for up to 3 months. Label and date the containers clearly before putting them into the freezer. Remove any fat that has hardened on the surface before reheating the stock.

LAMB STOCK: Prepare the stock as described above substituting lamb for some or all of the beef above.

VEGETABLE BROTH

MAKES ABOUT 2 QUARTS

2 tsp olive or corn oil

1 to 2 garlic cloves, finely minced

2 tsp minced shallots

3 qt water

1 large onion, thinly sliced (about 1 ¼ cups)

*1 leek, white, light green, and dark green parts,
    trimmed and sliced (about 3 cups)*

1 celery stalk, thinly sliced (about ½ cup)

1 carrot, thinly sliced (about ⅓ cup)

1 parsnip, thinly sliced (about ⅓ cup)

1 cup thinly sliced broccoli stems

1 cup thinly sliced fennel (with some tops)

½ cup dry white wine or vermouth (optional)

1 tbsp salt, or to taste

4 to 5 whole black peppercorns

½ tsp juniper berries

1 bay leaf

1 sprig fresh thyme or ¼ tsp dried thyme

1. Heat the olive oil in a soup pot over medium heat. Add the garlic and shallots and cook, stirring frequently, until they are translucent, 3 to 4 minutes.

2. Add the remaining ingredients and bring slowly up to a simmer. Cook until the broth has a good flavor, about 1 hour.

3. Strain the broth through a colander or sieve and then allow it to cool completely before storing in the refrigerator.

FOND DE VEAU

Brown Veal Stock

MAKES ABOUT 2 QUARTS

7 lb veal bones, blanched

1 calf's or pig's foot, split and blanched (optional)

5 qt cold water

*4 cups mirepoix (2 cups chopped onion, 1 cup chopped
    carrot, 1 cup chopped celery)*

1½ cups dry white wine

2 cups seeded and chopped tomatoes

1 cup sliced mushrooms

½ head garlic

1 bouquet garni (page 179)

1. Preheat the oven to 425°F.

2. Roast the blanched bones and foot, if using, in the oven until they're browned, about 45 minutes. Remove them from the oven and place the browned bones and foot into a large stockpot. Add the cold water and bring it to a simmer over medium-low heat. Do not let the water boil!

3. Using the same pan that you used to roast the bones, heat the roasting tray on the stove over medium heat and add the mirepoix. Sauté until it's lightly browned, about 10 minutes. Be careful not to burn either the bones or the mirepoix or you'll have a bitter stock. Take the roasting tray off the heat, deglaze the pan with the wine, return it to the heat, and reduce the liquid by half.

4. Skim the surface of the stock; add the mirepoix to the stockpot (be sure to scrape out the pan.) Add the tomatoes, mushrooms, garlic, and bouquet garni

to the stock. Reduce the heat to low and simmer gently for 4 to 5 hours.

5. Strain the finished stock into a container and cool it down quickly over a bowl of ice. Store it, covered, in the refrigerator for 2 days or freeze it for up to 3 months.

FISH STOCK

Use only the bones from mild, lean white fish, such as halibut or sole, to make this broth. Shells from shrimp, crab, and lobsters can be substituted for the bones to prepare a crustacean broth.

MAKES ABOUT 2 QUARTS

2 tbsp vegetable oil

5 lb fish bones from lean, white fish

2 onions, thinly sliced (about 2 ½ cups)

2 leeks, white and light green parts, thinly sliced (about 2 ½ cups)

2 celery stalks, thinly sliced (about 1 cup)

1 cup white mushrooms or mushroom stems, thinly sliced (optional)

1 cup dry white wine (optional)

2 ½ qt cold water

10 black peppercorns

6 parsley stems

2 sprigs fresh thyme, tarragon, or dill

2 bay leaves

1. Heat the oil in a soup pot over low heat. Add the fish bones, onions, leeks, celery, and mushrooms, if using. Stir until all the ingredients are evenly coated with oil. Cover the pot and cook without stirring for about 5 minutes.

2. Add the wine, if using, and simmer until the volume of wine is reduced by half. Add the water, peppercorns, parsley stems, herbs, and bay leaves. Bring the broth just up to a simmer. Continue to simmer gently for 35 to 45 minutes.

3. Strain the broth through a sieve. Discard the solids. If the broth is not be used right away, cool it thoroughly before storing it in the refrigerator for up to 3 days or in the freezer for up to 6 weeks.

DEMI-GLACE AND GLACE

Demi-glace and glace (or meat glaze) are used to make sauces or to strengthen flavor in completed dishes.

To make demi-glaçe, reduce the brown veal stock by two-thirds. To make glace, reduce demi-glace by half. You can also buy good quality frozen demi-glace and glace in some markets. Follow the directions for use on the package.

SAUCE BÉCHAMEL

White Sauce or Cream Sauce

2 tbsp unsalted butter

¼ cup all-purpose flour

1 cup milk

1 small bay leaf

1 small onion

1 clove

Salt and white pepper as needed

1. Melt the butter in a heavy-bottomed saucepan. Add the flour and cook for 30 seconds on low heat to

make a roux. Take the pan off the heat and add the milk. Whisk until the roux is dissolved and there are no lumps. Return the pan to medium heat, and stir the sauce continuously with a wooden spoon. The sauce will thicken as it comes to a boil. Stir the sauce as necessary while it simmers to smooth out the sauce and to keep the sauce from sticking to the pan as it cooks. Reduce the heat to low, and let the sauce simmer.

2. Secure the bay leaf onto the onion with the clove. (We refer to this as an *oignon piqué.*) Add it to the sauce and cover the pot tightly. Place the pot in a larger pan and add enough boiling water to the larger pan to rise to a height equal to or above the level of sauce in the pot.

3. Allow the water bath to simmer for 30 minutes. Stir the sauce twice during this cooking period. This method prevents the sauce from burning and produces a rich, creamy sauce. Season with salt and pepper to taste. Keep the sauce warm in the water bath right up until you're ready to use it, or you can cool the sauce and keep it in the refrigerator for up to 4 days.

MORNAY SAUCE

Add 1½ cups grated Gruyère cheese, 1 tsp Dijon mustard, and 1 large egg yolk to warm sauce béchamel and stir until the cheese has melted and the sauce is smooth. Season with nutmeg, salt, and pepper.

CHEF'S NOTE: If you've made the sauce in advance up to this point and stored it in the refrigerator, warm it up gently. A water bath is the safest option, but you can also use the stovetop: First, put a very thin layer of water in a heavy-bottomed saucepan. Add the béchamel and put the pot over very low heat. Let the sauce soften, stirring it once in a while. When the sauce is warm enough to stir easily,

increase the heat and bring it to a boil. You may need to add a bit of milk or cream to thin the sauce.

CRÊPES

MAKES 8 CRÊPES

2 cups all-purpose flour

½ teaspoon salt

2 cups milk

2 large eggs

1 tablespoon butter, melted

Melted butter or vegetable oil to coat pan, as needed

1. Sift the flour and salt together into a mixing bowl. Make a well in the center of the flour mixture.

2. In a separate bowl, blend the milk, eggs, and butter. Add the milk mixture to the flour mixture and stir by hand just until the batter is smooth. Let the batter rest in the refrigerator at least 1 and up to 12 hours before preparing the crêpes. Strain the batter if necessary to remove lumps before preparing the crêpes.

3. Heat a crêpe pan or small skillet over medium-high heat. Brush with melted butter. Pour about ¼ cup batter into the crêpe pan, swirling and tilting the pan to coat the bottom with batter. Cook until the first side is set and has a little color, about 2 minutes. Adjust the temperature under the pan if necessary. Use a thin metal or heatproof rubber spatula to lift the crêpe and turn it over. Cook on the other side until the crêpe is cooked through, 1 minute more.

DESSERT CRÊPES: Add ¼ cup sugar and ½ teaspoon vanilla extract to the batter.

Vanilla Sugar

Scented sugars are a great way to add a subtle aroma to your desserts. To make vanilla sugar, fill a jar with granulated sugar. Bury a vanilla bean in the sugar, cap the jar tightly, and let the sugar rest for a few days before using. You can use a fresh vanilla bean or you can use a vanilla bean that you steeped in milk or cream while preparing a custard or pastry cream.

Rolling Out Dough

Working with one piece of the dough at a time, unwrap the dough, place it on a lightly floured work surface, and scatter a little flour over the top. Use the least possible amount of flour to prevent the dough from sticking as you work.

Lightly flour your rolling pin. Use a back-and-forth motion to roll the dough, and give the dough a quarter turn periodically to maintain a round shape. If you are rolling out a rectangle or square shape, roll the dough lengthwise first and then across the width. As the rectangle or square increases in size, roll the pin on an angle into the corners to keep the sides straight.

Lift the dough periodically and dust the work surface, if necessary, to keep the dough from sticking. The dough should be between ⅛ and 1/16 of an inch thick, depending upon your recipe. It should be large enough to completely cover the bottom and sides of the pan.

To check the size and shape of your dough, gently set the pan you want to line in the center of the rolled out dough. The dough, whether a circle, square, or rectangle, should be the same dimensions as the pan, plus a margin of about 1 or 2 inches (depending up the height of the pan's sides).

Lining the Pan with Dough

For large crusts, roll the pastry loosely around the rolling pin to lift it to the pan. Let the pastry roll off the pin and into the pan. Smaller pieces can be carefully lifted and set into tartlet pans. Ease the dough into the pan, making sure that the sides and the rim are evenly covered. Press the dough gently against the sides and bottom.

Trim the overhanging dough to ¼ to ½ inch for tart pans, depending upon the size of the pan. In general, the larger your pan, the more overhang you should have. Tuck the dough overhang under itself and flute the edges for a raised edge, such as you make for a quiche (recipes pages 60–61). For tartlet pans, trim the dough even with the edge of the pan. Return the pastry to the refrigerator to firm up before baking blind, about 15 minutes.

Baking Blind

Preheat the oven to 400°F. Prick the dough evenly over the bottom and sides with the tines of a table fork. For quiche crusts, line the dough with a piece of parchment or waxed paper and fill about ½ full with pie weights, dry beans, or rice. For tartlet molds, either line with paper and weights or set a second pan on top of the filled pan, and place the shells on a baking sheet upside down. Bake just until the edges of the dough appear dry, but have not taken on any color. Remove the weights and paper. Cool to room temperature in the pan on a rack, and then fill and bake as directed in the recipe.

To pre-bake the crust completely, bake until the crust is set and dry, 12 to 15 minutes. Remove the pan from the oven and remove the paper and pie weights.

Return the crust to the oven and bake until the crust is completely dry and a light golden brown. Cool the crust to room temperature before adding a filling.

STORING DOUGH TO USE LATER

To store any leftover dough, pat the dough into flat disks or blocks and put them disk in a zip-close bag, pressing out as much air as possible before sealing the bag. It will hold 3 to 4 days in the refrigerator or up to 2 months in freezer.

Another option for freezing the dough is to roll it out and fit it into a disposable aluminum pie pan. Crimp the edges as you would normally, then prepare it for freezing as follows. To keep the crust well covered, line it with a piece of plastic wrap or waxed paper. Set a second pie plate inside the shell, and then wrap well with plastic wrap, using freezer tape or a zipper-close bag to keep the wrap from coming loose.

USING FROZEN PASTRY DOUGHS

Thaw frozen pastry doughs, whether homemade or purchased, in the refrigerator, letting the dough soften just until it becomes pliable but is still cool to the touch.

Keep the dough chilled, taking out only the amount you will work with during a short period of time. If the dough becomes too warm as you are rolling it out, the butter in between the thin layers will begin to melt into the flour, making the finished pastry gummy and less flaky.

Use a sharp knife when cutting and shaping the dough. Clean cuts ensure even rising. If you need to roll the dough to make it thinner, use gentle, even pressure and avoid running your roller over the edge of the dough. Refrigerate the dough after forming and before baking. Chilling helps keep the layers distinct, ensuring the best rise in the oven and flakiness in the finished dish.

PÂTE BRISÉE

MAKES 12 OUNCES

½ cup cold unsalted butter, cubed

1⅓ cups all-purpose flour

1 large egg yolk

3 tbsp ice-cold water

1. Preheat the oven to 375°F. Rub the butter into the flour until a light, sandy texture is achieved; you should have small pieces of butter within the mixture. These will give the pastry a flaky texture when it's cooked.

2. Mix the egg yolk with the water and pour it over the flour mixture. With an open hand, work the moisture into the mix until all of it becomes a little sticky, and then simply push it together to form a fairly firm, but not dry ball. Rest the dough in the refrigerator for at least 1 hour.

3. Roll the pastry dough out to ⅛-inch thickness, and line a 9-inch tart mold with the dough. Make sure you have no pleats or breaks in the pastry. Pierce the dough with a fork to prevent bubbling.

4. Line the tart with parchment paper and fill it with dried beans or peas. Blind bake the tart for 10 to 30 minutes, or until golden brown. Remove the parchment paper and beans from the tart, and return the tart to the oven to evenly brown the dough, approximately another 5 minutes.

5. Check the pastry thoroughly for any cracks or holes. Repair these by brushing them with an egg wash and placing the tart back in the oven for about 1 minute to cook the egg; this will seal the hole.

PÂTE SUCRÉE
Sweet Paste

MAKES 1½ POUNDS

1 cup unsalted butter

½ cup sugar

1 large egg, lightly beaten

1¾ cups all-purpose flour

1. Cream the butter and sugar together in a mixer, using the beater attachment, 5 to 10 minutes or until pale in color.

2. Add the egg and continue beating for 5 more minutes; scrape down the sides of the bowl a couple of times.

3. Switch to the slowest speed on the mixer and fold in the flour; mix until a soft paste is formed (do not overmix). Remove from the bowl and shape into a flat, 1-inch-thick slab. Wrap it in parchment paper.

4. Store the slab in the refrigerator for up to a week or in the freezer for 3 months.

NOTE: The paste must rest in the fridge for at least 1 hour before using.

PUFF PASTRY

This recipe produces something professionals refer to as blitz puff pastry. It is as flaky and buttery as the classic puff pastry, but you can put it together quickly. The rolling and folding process may appear lengthy, but most of that time is taken up by letting the dough chill enough to handle easily. Double or even triple the recipe if you like. For larger batches, you can use a stand mixer with a dough hook to blend the dough. Divide the dough into smaller pieces before wrapping and freezing to have your own pastry dough on hand to make sweet and savory pastries.

MAKES 2 POUNDS OF DOUGH

1⅔ cups butter, cubed and chilled

3 cups all-purpose flour

1½ tsp salt

1 cup cold water

1. Cut the butter into ¼-inch cubes. Refrigerate until chilled and firm.

2. Combine the flour and salt in a large mixing bowl. Add the butter and toss with your fingertips until the butter is coated with flour. Add all but about 2 tablespoons of the cold water. Mix with a pastry blender or a table fork until an evenly moist but still rough dough forms.

3. Cover the dough tightly with plastic wrap. Cool in the refrigerator until the butter is firm but not brittle, about 20 minutes.

4. Turn the dough out onto a lightly floured work surface. Roll it into a rectangle approximately 12 by 30 inches; the dough should be about ½ inch thick.

5. Fold the dough in thirds like a letter (this is the first of four 3-folds). Turn the dough 90 degrees so that the long end is once again parallel to the edge of your work surface. Roll the dough out to a rectangle as described above and fold once more (this is the second of four 3-folds). Wrap the dough tightly in

plastic wrap and chill for 30 minutes in the refrigerator. Continue rolling and folding the dough for the third and fourth 3-folds as describe above, chilling the dough in between folds if necessary.

6. After completing the final 3-fold, wrap the dough in plastic wrap and allow it to firm under refrigeration for at least 1 hour before using. The dough will last up to 1 week in the refrigerator or it may be frozen for up to 2 months.

PÂTE À CHOU
Chou Paste

MAKES 2 POUNDS

½ cup unsalted butter

1¼ cups cold water

1½ cups all-purpose flour, sifted

Optional flavorings (see note)

5 large eggs, lightly beaten

1. Melt the butter in a medium saucepan over low heat. Pour the water in and bring it to a boil. Take the pan off the heat and add the sifted flour. Beat it with a wooden spoon until it's smooth, 30 to 60 seconds.

2. Return the pan to low heat for 1 minute to dry out the mixture; stir it constantly. Take the pan off the heat and allow the mixture to cool for 5 minutes.

3. If you choose to add flavorings, add them now. Gradually add the beaten eggs a little at a time, beating thoroughly between additions, until you have a shiny paste that can hold its shape when piped or spooned. (You may find that you have not used all of the egg; that is okay. If your paste is a little dry, you may want to beat another egg and add some or all of it to make the right consistency.)

4. Store the paste covered in the refrigerator until it's needed.

CHEF'S NOTE: Chou paste is best used the day it's made. It must go through a drying period when baking. Once you've baked it to the desired color, turn the oven down by half and dry the chou for 15 to 20 minutes. This allows the remaining water to evaporate so the chou can maintain its shape when removed from the oven to cool. You can add flavorings to the pâte à chou, such as 1 pinch citrus zest, 1 teaspoon vanilla extract, or 1 tablespoon flavored cordials or liqueurs.

CRÈME PÀTISSIÈRE
Pastry Cream

MAKES 1 POUND

2 cups milk, divided use

3 large egg yolks

¼ cup cornstarch

⅓ cup sugar, divided use

½ vanilla bean

2 tbsp unsalted butter

Whipped cream (optional)

Flavorings (optional): 2 tbsp kirsch, brandy, Cointreau, or other cordials and liqueurs

1. In a medium bowl, mix ½ cup of the milk with the egg yolks, cornstarch, and half the sugar to make a slurry. Mix with a whisk until it's smooth and the cornstarch has dissolved, about 1 minute.

2. Heat the remaining 1½ cups of the milk, sugar,

and the vanilla bean in a medium saucepan over medium heat until it's boiling. Pour the boiling milk onto the slurry while whisking. Return this mixture to the milk pan.

3. Cook the mix out over medium heat, stirring with a wooden spoon until lumps begin to form, about 5 minutes. (This is one of the few dishes in cooking where lumps are accepted.) Just continue to stir over the heat and eventually all of those lumps will become one thick mass.

4. Beat the mix with a wooden spoon over low heat until smooth, for about 1 minute. Pour the pastry cream into a bowl and dot it with butter. Move the bowl around until the butter melts and coats the top of the cream. This will prevent a skin from forming.

5. When the cream is cooled and the butter is still liquid, beat them together to combine them. Cover and store it in the refrigerator for up to 3 days.

6. To prepare the crème pâtisserie to serve or to use as a filling, beat the cream in a mixer until soft and smooth. See the notes below for finishing and flavoring options.

FINISHING OPTIONS

Crème pâtisserie is a standard filling for cream puffs and éclairs. and is also used as the basis of several desserts, including Bavarian creams and mousse. To make them, fold whipped cream into the softened crème. If you add about 1 cup whipped cream for every 3 cups of crème, you'll have a lighter texture and a richer flavor. If you add more whipped cream, say up to a 50-50 blend of crème and whipped cream,

it will be more like a mousse. If you add a bit of softened and melted gelatin to the mousse, you'll have a Bavarian cream that you can chill and unmold before you serve it.

You can add flavorings to the pastry cream, whether or not you want to include whipped cream. Classic options include Grand Marnier, Kahlua, Amaretto, or Kirschwasser. Add these flavorings to taste, but remember that if you add more than a tablespoon for every half cup, you may thin the crème more than you'd like.

SAUCE AU CHOCOLAT
Chocolate Sauce

Use the best chocolate you can afford. The higher the fat content, the more luscious it will be.

ABOUT 1 CUP; SERVES 6

¾ cup half-and-half

3 tbsp sugar

6 oz dark chocolate, chopped

2 tbsp unsalted butter

Bring the half-and-half and sugar to a boil in a medium saucepan. Once it reaches a boil immediately remove from the heat. Add the melted chocolate and stir it thoroughly. Bring the sauce back to a simmer for about 1 minute. Remove it from the heat and whisk in the butter to form a rich, smooth chocolate sauce. Use now or store in the refrigerator for up to 3 days; rewarm gently before serving.

APRICOT GLAZE

MAKES ¾ CUP GLAZE

¾ cup apricot jam

7 tsp sugar

1 tbsp apricot brandy (optional)

Boil the jam and sugar together in a medium sauce-pan over medium heat until it's liquid, about 5 minutes. Add the brandy, if using, and pour the glaze through a fine sieve. Set it aside.

SAUCE D'ABRICOT
Apricot Sauce

This sauce is deliciously versatile. It can be served warm or chilled, and goes well with a variety of desserts. We recommend serving this sauce over ice cream, with *mousse au chocolat,* on *charlotte aux pommes,* or peach and goat cheese tart, and, of course, with hot beignets.

SERVES 6

1 heaping cup dried apricots

2 cups water

⅓ cup sugar

Zest and juice of ½ lemon

2 tbsp apricot brandy

¼ cup apricot jam

Place all of the ingredients into a blender and mix on high speed until smooth. Pass the sauce through a fine-mesh strainer and serve.

Index

JOHN W. FISCHER has more than 20 years experience in the restaurant industry. He has held management as well as sommelier positions at such top New York City restaurants as Mondrian and was Cellar Master at the Rainbow Room. He holds an Advanced Certificate from the Wine & Spirit Education Trust and is the author of *At Your Service: A Hands-on Guide to the Professional Dining Room*. A 1988 graduate of The Culinary Institute of America, he returned to join the faculty in 2000, and is now associate professor in table service.

LOU JONES hails from the United Kingdom. A master at his craft, he has garnered a number of awards, including British National Chef of the Year in 1994, two Culinary Olympics gold medals in 1992, gold medals at the Culinary World Cup in 1990 and 1994, and was appointed a member of the Most Excellent Order of the British Empire in 1994. He currently assistant dean of culinary arts at The Culinary Institute of America.

A Note on the Type

This book was set in Adobe Garamond Premier Pro.
Noted type designer Robert Slimbach, creator of the original Adobe
Garamond, received a rare opportunity to revisit his arguably most well-known
typeface design. Following a thorough reexamination of some of Claude Garamond's
original type designs and metal punches at a museum in Antwerp, Belgium, Slimbach
began formulating plans for a new digital typeface based on Garamond's designs,
encompassing what he observed there. The result was a full-featured modern
composition family designed for versatility in a variety of mediums and
printing situations, and offering a different, yet equally important,
interpretation of the work of one of sixteenth-century France's
most significant type designers.

Art direction, design, and composition by Kevin Hanek

Printed in Singapore by Imago Worldwide Printing